In Search of
Persons
of PEACE

Inspirational Stories of How
Ordinary People Influence
Multitudes for Christ

Carolyn Leslie Knight

OMS · ONE MISSION SOCIETY

http://oms.media

In Search of Persons of Peace – Carolyn Leslie Knight

Edited by Barbara Potter

Printed in the United States of America

One Mission Society
P.O. Box A
Greenwood, Indiana 46142

317.888.3333

www.onemissionsociety.org
http://oms.media

Paperback ISBN: 978-1-62245-310-8

eBook ISBN: 978-1-62245-311-5

10 9 8 7 6 5 4 3 2 1

Available where books are sold.

Contents

Every Community for Christ

Every Community for Christ (ECC) is the worldwide evangelistic church multiplication catalyst of One Mission Society, serving through biblically based teams in more than sixty countries. Every Community for Christ works within the context of partnership with denominations or church associations to start church-planting movements among the nations.

Every Community for Christ ministry teams work to give every man, woman, boy, and girl an opportunity to hear the good news of Jesus and respond in faith. Partnerships are formed to evangelize, plant churches, and train leaders for multiplication. The intent is to glorify God by helping people experience new life in Christ in the context of a healthy local church.

Before entering a village, town, city, or neighborhood, ECC teams pray that the Holy Spirit will lead them to a person of peace. The teams are responsible for praying, evangelizing, discipling, forming worship groups and churches, training leaders, and modeling the way, all the while equipping new believers to repeat the process. Each team engages in culturally relevant, lovingly appropriate, and intensely systematic personal soul winning and discipleship with the intention of incorporating new believers into new, multiplying congregations.

Every Community for Christ is always looking for committed believers who would like to be a part of this ministry. For more information, call One Mission Society at 317-888-3333 or go to the website at *www.onemissionsociety.org.*

Chapter 1

The Santal People of India

O h, Thakur Jiu, will you stay hidden from us forever? Please let me know you," the old man Kolean prayed again and again.

Kolean was an elder and a sage among the Santal people, a group of two and a half million people living in a region north of Calcutta, India. To the Santal, Thakur Jiu is the maker of all creation. He sees everything and has set everything in its place. He nourishes all, great and small. He is distinct and is not to be seen with earthly eyes.

Ages ago, however, as the Santal people multiplied and began to spread upon the earth, they tried to migrate north to find more room for their people. They encountered a mountain range and could not find a way to cross. The Santal tried many times, but the way was too rough and steep. They cried out to Thakur Jiu for help, but they still could not cross the mountains. They believed that demons were causing their troubles, so the Santal people decided to make a pact with the demons: the Santal would turn from Thakur Jiu and worship the demons if they successfully crossed the mountains. They did find a pass through the mountains soon after, and from that time on, they began to worship the demons. Thakur Jiu was slowly forgotten.

In 1867, Lars Skrefsrud, a pioneer missionary from Norway,

and his Danish friend, Hans Borreson, found the Santal people as they were ministering in India. The men worked hard to learn their language and prayed for receptive people among the Santal who would believe the message of salvation. As soon as he was able, Lars began to preach to them about the one true God. He was preaching in a village when he heard an old man talking in the crowd.

"I think this stranger must be talking to us about Thakur Jiu," said Kolean excitedly. "This must mean that Thakur Jiu has not forgotten us after all!"

In learning the language of the Santal people, Lars discovered that *Thakur Jiu* meant "genuine god." Could the Thakur Jiu of the Santal be the same God in heaven that Lars served? Lars knew that he had to learn more about Thakur Jiu, and he saw immediately that Kolean might be a potential believer. The two men began a relationship in their search for God together.

The more the men talked in the days to come, the more Lars was convinced that Kolean was describing the God of the Bible, because the creation and flood stories Kolean shared with Lars were so similar to the biblical account. But Lars was confused. If the Santal believed in Thakur Jiu, the one true God, then why did they still worship demons?

"Our forefathers knew Thakur Jiu and worshiped him long ago," Kolean explained. He went on to say that his people feared that Thakur Jiu would never care about them or have anything more to do with them because of the horrible way their forefathers had sinned. Kolean also told Lars that the Santal people longed to know Thakur Jiu again and that they still knew he was the one true God.

Lars then shared the good news with Kolean right away. Lars told him how all the peoples of the world had sinned and how Thakur Jiu sent his own Son to die as a sacrifice for all our wrongdoings. Lars told Kolean that he and all the Santal could have forgiveness and a new relationship with Thakur Jiu. Kolean's face lit up with joy to learn that Thakur Jiu still loved them and had never forgotten them. He could hardly contain himself to learn that God wanted all the Santal to live with him forever in a perfect place where no one would ever be sick or hurt again.

Kolean immediately vowed his allegiance to Thakur Jiu and to his Son, Jesus. Kolean prayed to the Lord, repented of his sins, and received Jesus as his Savior and Master. Together the missionaries and Kolean began to tell the good news to all the people. With Kolean's help as a respected elder and sage, the missionaries were able to bridge the gap between the Bible and the beliefs that the Santal already had. Thousands of Santal begged to be reconciled to Thakur Jiu through Jesus. Lars and Hans were soon baptizing eighty people per day.

Lars baptized fifteen thousand people during his thirty years in India, and he also translated the Bible into the language of the Santal people. With the help of other believers, eighty-five thousand Santal people came to Christ in the following years. Thousands more kept coming to Christ over the next several decades.

God knew that Kolean was seeking to be reconciled back to him and would be receptive to the truth, so he arranged the providential meeting for him with Lars and Hans. Kolean was a man of reputation as an elder and a sage of the Santal, so God knew he would be able to influence many others to hear and to believe. The Lord also knew that, with his passion for God and truth, Kolean would become active in referring people to him.

A person of peace is born.

Persons of Peace

The purpose of this book is to motivate and challenge you to get in on the exciting search for persons of peace and to inspire you to witness for Christ more than ever before. Like Kolean, an elder among the Santal people of India, you may have people living near you who do not understand the good news of salvation. They may have been briefly exposed to the Gospel, but they do not understand enough to make a decision for Christ. These people may be confused about who God is and what he is like, and yet they may also be hungry to know him. In the midst of the problems and chaos of their lives, will you be one the Lord can use to help fill in the gaps of their understanding? Will you point them clearly to the only way of salvation through Jesus? Will you discover the next person of peace who could influence many others to do the same?

How Did the Term *Person of Peace* Originate?

The concept of *persons of peace* comes directly from Scripture. In the Gospels of Matthew (10:1-42), Mark (6:7-13), and Luke (9:1-6; 10:1-24), you will find accounts of how Jesus sends messengers two by two to proclaim the kingdom of God and to heal the sick. Jesus gives specific instructions about what kind of person the messengers should look for to help them in their work. In Luke 10:5-6, Jesus tells his messengers: *But whatever house you enter, first say, 'Peace to this house.' And if a son of peace is there, your peace will rest on it; if not, it will return to you.*

Why was it important that a man of peace be present in that house? In Luke 10:3, we have a clue when Jesus says, *Go your way; behold, I send you out as lambs among wolves.* Jesus knows that he is sending out his people to do a dangerous job. They may encounter hostility and opposition, but they are to return this negative response with love and gentleness. Having a person of peace in the community to support them would be a blessing for their work and would reflect the way that Jesus wants them to interact with the communities.

How Does a Person of Peace Differ from an Unbeliever?

A *person of peace* is different from other terms used by believers – such as *seekers*, *unbelievers*, or *the lost* – because these words refer only to individual persons and not to the people they can influence. Too often believers have seen the rescue of a lost soul as an end in itself. If a person came to know the Lord, it was a victory won for only that person: end of story. But the concept that Jesus was teaching is so much greater. A person of peace is not only an individual in need of salvation but one who is also connected to a household, a family, or a community in the same need. A person of peace has the potential to be a bridge to many others. Believers miss many opportunities along the way when they do not see new believers as immediate bridges to all those to whom they are connected. Acknowledging each person's sphere of influence is so important to understanding the concept of persons of peace.

Who Is a Person of Peace?

While the concept of a person of peace is only mentioned specifically in one passage of Scripture, there are many examples of such people throughout the Bible. Based on these examples, certain characteristics can be deduced. Persons of peace are people God has prepared ahead of time to be receptive to the Gospel, the good news of Jesus Christ. They welcome the messengers that God sends their way, and they even try to serve or assist the messengers in some way, especially in spreading the Gospel further. Persons of peace may be unbelievers who have great potential to be used in furthering God's kingdom. They have three defining qualities in their lives. These qualities are:

1. *Being receptive to the Gospel.* The Bible describes a person of peace as someone who is receptive to the

messenger. In Matthew 10:40, Jesus says, *"He who receives you receives Me, and he who receives Me receives Him who sent Me."* A person of peace welcomes the messengers, provides food and lodging, and is open to hearing Jesus' message. Jesus instructs the messengers to bless this person of peace and his home. On the other hand, to those who do not welcome the messengers of Christ, Jesus instructs them: *"when you depart from there, shake off the dust under your feet as a testimony against them"* (Mark 6:11).

2. *Being well-known.* Persons of peace should have a reputation – either good or bad – in the community. The important qualities to have are name recognition and the capability to influence other people. They are men or women who are known in the area, and they are respected, feared, or even disdained. Cornelius, an important Roman centurion described in Acts 10, is a good example of this characteristic.

3. *Being connected.* Persons of peace are individuals who are connected with other people and are willing to refer their acquaintances to the messengers. They bring family and friends together in the community to hear the Gospel message. They are also people who eagerly refer others to Jesus. They tell their story of salvation in the hope that others will receive Jesus also. The story of the woman at the well in John 4 is a powerful example of this characteristic. The woman embraced the Gospel message and immediately invited her entire community to come and hear Jesus.

These three characteristics will be evident in each person of peace you encounter. While you may meet people who exhibit one or two qualities, all three qualities must be present in order to identify someone as a person of peace.

The rest of this book includes many examples of people who show the three qualities of persons of peace. The stories tell about scriptural, historical, and present-day people and represent what has been observed over and over in a person of peace. The stories also demonstrate God's providence in arranging meetings between witnesses who are yearning to sow the seeds of the Gospel and the persons of peace who are seeking to know the one true God – like the meeting between Lars and Kolean.

How Do I Get Started?

There is no greater adventure than searching for persons of peace. The search may lead you to your next-door neighbor who is suicidal from depression or addicted to painkillers. It may lead you to the teenager who attends church because all of his friends go, but he doesn't understand what he hears. It may lead you to the full-time-working single mom who is exhausted and wondering about the meaning of life. It may take you to the successful business man whose wife just walked out with the children. It may even take you to a country or culture far away from your present home.

Persons of peace are everywhere, and you will meet them every week. Regardless of your location, adventures await you if you are simply willing to "go and tell." Why not put on the full armor of God and become a messenger for the King? Why not tell Jesus today that you are choosing to obey his command to make disciples of all nations? Why not be used as a light bearer for Jesus? Ask God to help you in this mission to find persons of peace and then do it.

Chapter 2

On-the-Job Training

I n my personal search for persons of peace, I never stop learn-ing. In every encounter I have with people, I gather new information about how to go about reaching the lost and finding persons of peace in the community. Sometimes I learn from positive experiences, and sometimes I learn the hard way in more difficult situations. I think you will find this to be true for you also. Part of the adventure is discovering that God uses every situation for our good and his glory. I would like to share some of my own on-the-job training experiences with you to help you prepare the way for your own journey.

Don't Be Surprised at Who Becomes a Person of Peace

One early lesson I had to learn about bringing people to the Lord is that God may bring the most unlikely people into your path to use as persons of peace. At the age of nineteen, I was introduced to my ministry by working at a homeless shelter in Seattle, Washington. A Native American woman named Willie Shoulderblade came in every day. She was one of the hundreds of homeless people on skid row. Usually she was intoxicated, and the drunker she was, the meaner she became. It was not unusual, on these occasions, for her to be forcefully escorted out of the shelter because she would start fights and create chaos. By chaos, I don't mean heated arguments. I mean chair-throwing, hair-pulling, eye-gouging, rolling-on-the-floor fights. One night, during an evening service, she threw a Bible at the preacher as hard as she could. The startled man just ducked and kept on preaching. You never knew what Willie was going to do next. I shared the Gospel with Willie again and again. She rejected it over and over.

Willie suffered greatly from her life of drunkenness and sin on the streets. One day, in the winter, she walked barefooted on a sheet of ice for more than a dozen city blocks to get to our mission. Her feet were frozen, and I gently washed them in a pan of warm water and rubbed them to get back the circulation. A man had stolen her shoes during the night. Our mission was home to Willie. Although she rejected our message, she always knew she could come there and receive love and hugs as well as a hot meal and fresh clothing. She knew she could count on us.

"Please give Jesus a chance, Willie," I begged her. "You are going to get killed on these streets. Jesus has a better life for you if you will follow him."

"You might as well stop talking to me about Jesus," she replied. "He can't help me." But she kept coming back to the mission, so I didn't stop talking to her. I will admit, though, that I didn't think Willie would ever become a Christian.

Another night she came to the mission, and blood was running down her legs. She practically fell into the doorway. We took her to the nearest emergency room, and we learned she was having a miscarriage. She had gotten pregnant by a homeless man. She explained that he didn't want the baby and had kicked her in the stomach repeatedly.

"Oh, Willie," I said again. "This is no life for you. Jesus loves you and he will give you a new life if you will let him."

"That Jesus stuff would never work for me," she replied doubtfully.

If there were one person I could never imagine getting saved, it was Willie. I could see her only as she was, not as God saw her. But I didn't stop loving Willie, and I didn't stop talking to her. One day, to my surprise, she came in sober. She had finally come to the end of herself and could not bear life any longer. She heard yet another Gospel message, but this time she came to the altar to pray. Right then and there she accepted Christ as her Savior. I was astounded, and when she finished praying, she said, "But what about my drinking? I need help to stop drinking."

We prayed with her again, and Willie was completely delivered from alcoholism from that day forward. I never saw a person change so much. She soon had a little apartment, and then she got a job working at the same hospital where she had miscarried months earlier. She changed from being a surly drunk into a joyful witness of God's salvation and power to everyone she met. She witnessed powerfully to others on the streets.

The story of Willie Shoulderblade illustrates the power of God to make any person a new creation in him. I never pictured Willie as a potential bridge to others for the Gospel, but God could see the potential in her all along. I also learned so much about the search for the lost in her changed life. I learned not to give up on someone. I learned not to look at a person's outward appearance and circumstances. And I learned to keep sowing the seeds of the Gospel faithfully and to leave the results to the Lord. He is able.

Divine Appointments Can Happen Anywhere

I lived in Kampala, Uganda, during the early '90s, and frequently on Tuesdays one or two women and I would go out searching for persons of peace. We did a variety of things in our searching:

knocked on doors, stood on a busy corner, or entered shops looking for people with whom to share the Gospel.

One day, we passed a little grocery store, and I felt a nudge in my spirit to go inside. I knew it was the Holy Spirit directing my steps. The colorful Rainbow Supermarket sign glared out at me as if it were lit up in neon lights. The store was empty except for the storeowner, a lovely lady named Lydia. Dressed in a brightly colored kanga (the wrap-around skirt so common in East Africa), she was busy stocking shelves during a quiet moment when no customers were around – yet another confirmation that this may have been a divine appointment.

I greeted her, introduced my friend, and began a conversation with Lydia. As we chatted, I learned that Lydia had been attending church, so I asked her whether she believed she would go to heaven. She said no and continued to explain that she was trying to do good things. She prayed sometimes, but she was fearful of death and hoped that God would let her into heaven. I asked her whether I could show her from God's Word how she could know for sure that she would go to heaven, and she readily agreed. I went through the plan of salvation with her, and she eagerly prayed with me and told me that she knew that she was now born again.

As we talked further, Lydia's eyes filled with tears as she told me that she had a daughter, Sarah, aged ten, who was terminally ill. She said that she had taken her to see many doctors but none could help her. The rate of HIV was over 20 percent at that time in Uganda, so I wondered if her little girl was suffering from the ravages of that disease. Most doctors didn't give an HIV diagnosis because of the superstitious belief that if you said the words out loud, a word curse would fall on the person, and you were dooming them to certain death. I was sensitive to the stigma of that disease, so I just listened and didn't speculate as to the type or cause of her illness.

Lydia's voice broke as she told us that Sarah could no longer go to school and that she was afraid to die because she didn't know whether she would go to heaven. Lydia felt that she couldn't offer words of comfort to her daughter because she didn't understand until that moment what salvation meant. Lydia asked me to call her little girl and tell her just what I had explained to her. Lydia said, "I know she will want to be saved just as I was."

I assured her that I would call Sarah that afternoon. When I called, she sounded raspy and weak, and I could barely hear her voice. I slowly and simply explained the plan of salvation to her, and she also said that she would like to pray. She strained to whisper a simple sinner's prayer and repeated the words after me. I could tell it was a tremendous effort on her part to say those few sentences. Then I asked her if she knew that now she was saved, and she softly whispered, "Yes." I told her that her name was now written in the Book of Life and that she need not fear for her future. I told her that even now there were angels in heaven rejoicing over her. I could feel her smiling through the phone lines.

Sarah died soon after that phone call. I know that God's angels escorted her to Jesus. I praise God that he led me into that little store. I did follow-up visits for discipleship with Lydia many times after that incident, and she always greeted me with a joyous smile and a warm hug. Lydia demonstrated the actions of a true person of peace because her first action as a brand new Christian was to connect me with her daughter, who also needed salvation. Lydia said that Sarah died peacefully in her faith, and for that she would be eternally grateful.

The death of Sarah also brought about many opportunities for Lydia to share her testimony of salvation with friends and relatives. She gave a glowing account of her salvation as well as Sarah's to those who came to offer condolences in the days and weeks after the funeral. She loved to tell the story of how Sarah died so peacefully because she knew that she was going to heaven.

I watched how the Lord helped Lydia take what could have been the most painful event of her life and turn it into a powerful testimony of the peace and security that we can have through knowing Jesus. The sharing of the most difficult days of our lives may be what God can use the most in witnessing to others. What has God brought you through, and to whom can you tell your story?

I also learned that the Lord will guide our feet if we are open to his promptings. Each day can be an adventure in our walk of faith if we listen to his voice and make ourselves available to his call. Sometimes we may hear a still, small voice or an inner nudge, but he will lead us to open hearts if we are listening and willing to follow.

God Is at Work Even if We Can't See It

Another lesson I learned about the search for persons of peace occurred when I worked as a weekend houseparent at a safe house for teenaged boys. The boys were overflows from the overcrowded detention center or those who could not be placed in foster care. Many were gang members who already had long rap sheets that included drug dealing, armed robbery, and rape.

One night I was leading devotion time in the living room, as was our usual custom after dinner. I pleaded with the boys to turn their lives over to Jesus and spoke the phrase "crime doesn't pay." At that point, I was interrupted.

"Ms. Knight," one boy said. "We like you and you're a nice lady, but you really don't know what you're talking about. I could take you right now to a building, pull a board out of the wall, and show you a shoebox where I hid thirty-six thousand dollars from selling drugs. I think it pays pretty good!"

At his brash statement, all the boys burst out laughing. Then one after another, they started telling of their successful criminal activities – from stealing cool cars to robbing stores – and all the money they made from these activities. I tried to interrupt and get control of the group, but they drowned me out with bragging about their exploits. Finally, I gave up.

"Boys, please just think about what I said," I responded weakly as I left the room in defeat. I went next door to the laundry room, leaned over the washing machine, and began to cry. I cried out to the Lord and said, "Lord, I failed you so badly tonight. I didn't relate to the boys at all. If anything, I just made things worse. How can I get through to them, God?"

Suddenly, I heard a noise. A boy had opened the door and saw me crying and praying. He was bringing in some laundry. He looked startled and quickly dropped his clothes on the floor and left. Soon I heard silence in the living room, and I knew he had told the other boys what he had seen.

I wiped my face and went in to say good-night to the boys. They were extra nice, and everyone went to bed without any trouble. I thought that was the end of the situation, but I was awakened by a knock on my door at midnight by the night guard who said, "One of the boys can't sleep until he speaks with you. Do you want to talk to him?"

I found the boy in the living room. He was slumped over, and he was wiping tears. "What's going on?" I asked him.

"I just want to know why you would cry for me." He was dead serious.

The tears of my defeat were what had touched his heart. I told him that I cried because I cared for him so much, and that I cared so much because Jesus cared for *him* so much. He listened intently while I shared with him the plan of salvation and the love shown to him by Jesus' death on the cross.

In the middle of the night, that gang member became a

person of peace. His heart became receptive to the Gospel message. He was close to adulthood and had years to serve in prison, but before he was transferred out, I got to spend more time with him in discipleship and take him to church with me several times. He was markedly different in the safe house, and everyone heard his testimony before he left. He openly shared during devotion times in the evening and several times I watched him influence younger boys in telling about the difference Christ had made in his life.

I learned from that experience that our sharing with others may seem totally unsuccessful. We may even be laughed at and ridiculed. But God's Word is still having an effect, even when we can't see it. He can even use what we see as our failures to draw people to himself. Our job is to faithfully sow those seeds and to care enough to keep on sowing even if the seeds fall on seemingly hard and unyielding ground.

Love for Others Must Outweigh Our Fears

God definitely has a sense of humor, and I discovered that quality when I went to Tanzania, Africa. After months of traveling to churches to raise funds, saying all those tearful good-byes, and studying hard for nine months to learn Swahili, I finally arrived at my final destination. The challenges of life and ministry began immediately. I was surrounded by people who walked and biked everywhere in a confusing grid of roads that weren't listed on any map. I never knew where I was. A large percentage of the people were either Muslim or animist, and many were still going to witch doctors. I felt overwhelmed thinking about where to start doing evangelism.

Very few nationals spoke a word of English, and I often felt intimidated and unintelligent in doing the simplest things, such as buying food in the open market. Having to function completely in a new language often made me feel like a child. I would stumble through a request for rice and incorrectly count out the change using unfamiliar coins. One day I gave a lady the equivalent of thirty-two dollars instead of thirty-two cents for a single pineapple. That purchase was both a costly and an embarrassing mistake. Every night my brain felt exhausted from trying to speak and understand Swahili.

But each day, the Holy Spirit seemed to be telling me to "go out and witness." And I continued to respond that I was not ready and could barely function because I was not yet good enough in Swahili.

"Go out and witness," was his calm command. And I continued to provide more excuses.

Then one day I opened my Bible to 1 Corinthians 2:1-5. I couldn't believe the words. The Holy Spirit was talking directly to me when Paul said that he *did not come with excellence of speech or of wisdom declaring to you the testimony of God* (v. 1), but that he came to the people *in weakness, in fear, and in much trembling* (v. 3). Paul went on to say that his *speech and ... preaching were not with persuasive words of human wisdom, but in demonstration of the Spirit and of power* (v. 4). I don't ever remember reading this passage, and I was amazed to find that the apostle Paul felt exactly like I did – weak and fearful at the thought of speaking. Paul didn't come with superiority of speech, but he did come determined to share Jesus Christ and his crucifixion.

God needed me to understand that my presentation of the Gospel didn't have to be complex or perfect; it just needed to be sincere and Spirit led. I didn't have to be dynamic; I just needed to be true and to demonstrate love through the power of the Holy Spirit. With this perspective, I was ready to go.

That very morning, I picked up my Bible and headed out the door. I started down my dirt road, and I was determined to witness to the first person I saw. Maybe I would find a person of peace. Soon I spotted two teenaged boys leaning on a fence. I greeted them and began a conversation. As best I could, I found out about them, and they soon knew all that I could tell them in Swahili about myself and why I had come.

We laughed when I didn't say a word correctly, and they were kind and helped me with my pronunciation. Later that morning, I presented the Gospel to them. Yes, I made mistakes. I forgot some words, and I repeated myself, but I got the message out. To my great surprise, they both wanted to pray with me. I asked to meet with them again in a few days to begin studying the Bible, and as true persons of peace, they brought more teens and children with them. These people also prayed to have Jesus come into their hearts. The new children and youth bought friends with them the following week, and they too wanted to pray. We grew from two to seven to twelve to thirty believers in a short few weeks. The growth continued over the following months, and eventually, more than 100 people were attending the Bible study every week.

I learned from that experience that we must love people more than we fear making mistakes. We must love people in spite of feeling inadequate and intimidated. God will use us and work through our inabilities when we make ourselves available to him. Thankfully, I learned the amazing power of the principle of finding persons of peace who will become bridges to others around them.

Show Love Even to the Unlovable

A lesson I will never forget is one I learned about the search for persons of peace at an abortion clinic. I have been a sidewalk counselor for many years, and one day a group of us gathered at a clinic to pray that it would be shut down. It was in the middle of July and very hot. We arrived around eight in the morning and were soon sweating profusely on the black pavement of the parking lot. One of our ladies thought ahead and brought a jug of cold lemonade and some paper cups and stored them in the back of her car for us to use as needed.

We had not been at the abortion clinic for very long when a van pulled up. Out climbed thirteen witches in black robes with pentagrams hanging around their necks on chains. I thought, "This can't be happening. I am in the Bible belt of the United States." But it was real.

The witches walked in and among our group of prayers, and they started praying too. But they were praying to Father Lucifer, as they called him. One witch was standing near to me, and I heard her say clearly, "Oh, Father Lucifer, let the blood of the babies continue to flow. And let each death be as a sacrifice to you to give you more power over this city."

I was furious at hearing that prayer. The witches prayed louder and louder, trying to drown us out. We didn't know what to do, but we *did* know that we weren't going to walk away from the battlefield, so we all just kept praying. We were calling out to Jehovah God to shut that place of death down, and the witches were calling to Lucifer for the deaths to increase. I was reminded of the battle on Mount Carmel with Elijah and the priests of Baal (1 Kings 18).

Suddenly, without warning, one of the witches just hit the ground hard and lay still. My first thought was, "Oh my goodness, God has struck her dead." Then I thought with joy, "Wow! God has actually struck her dead." I wanted to break out dancing. Maybe God would strike them all dead, and they would start dropping like bowling pins, one after another.

Out of the corner of my eye, I saw one of my Christian brothers go running by me. I wondered what he was doing, but I didn't give it much thought. I was still feeling triumphantly victorious over my enemy. Then I saw him quickly returning with a cup of lemonade in his hand. My mouth dropped open as I watched that man kneel down by the witch, take her in his arms, and begin giving her sips of lemonade. She had passed out from the heat. I watched him perform that act of love, and I was forever changed.

You see, he didn't see an evil witch crying out for the blood sacrifices of children. He saw a fallen woman, blinded by Satan and in bondage to him. This gentleman was the only one in our group who remembered that, as lights in this world for the Master, we are to love our enemies and do good to those who persecute us.

The man continued to talk kindly to the young woman as I watched and learned from him. He even gave her a Gospel tract, and she accepted it – she, a practicing Satanist. She would never have taken a tract from me because I didn't show her love. I learned that our search for the lost must be lovingly done. Sometimes our acts of kindness, done in Jesus' name, may be the only tools that make people receptive to hearing the Gospel. I learned that even the one who seems to be the most evil on the outside may be ready on the inside to hear a message about Christ.

I believe this young woman indicated that she was a potential person of peace in accepting that Gospel tract. She was receptive in receiving the message of salvation that was contained in that little booklet. The witches left after this incident, but I know that a seed was sown in her heart that day. We prayed over the tract and asked the Lord to continue to speak to her through his Word.

OMS Has a Commitment to Persons of Peace

I work with One Mission Society (OMS), an international mission organization that is more than 100 years old. OMS has a vested interest in searching for persons of peace because the founders embraced this concept from the beginning. From the early 1900s, OMS carried out plans to evangelize entire nations – beginning with Japan – and not just small towns or individual regions. OMS organized evangelism teams that covered the entire nation of Japan in just a few years. To succeed in this goal, OMS made a commitment to finding persons of peace to help its evangelists reach communities throughout the entire country.

That early focus has not changed, and the present-day vision shines just as brightly. OMS missionaries and national partners regularly carry out evangelistic saturation projects for reaching people in specific regions. OMS has a fourfold focus that includes evangelism, church planting, leadership training, and forming strategic partnerships. Its Every Community for Christ ministry is training evangelists and church planters all over the world to bring people to a belief in Christ.

In 2013, more than one million souls were converted to Christ through OMS ministries in more than seventy countries. OMS missionaries and national partners planted forty thousand new worshiping groups or house churches in 2014, and the goal is sixty thousand for 2015. Thousands of national evangelists are equipped to understand the true meaning of *persons of peace*. New converts are immediately encouraged and equipped to give their testimony to everyone they know in their family, community, and work environment. By using persons of peace in the communities, OMS missionaries and national partners create a chain reaction of new believers who bring more souls into the kingdom. One new believer becomes a stream of salvation that can grow into a river as family and friends come to know the Lord. God is mightily at work in our world today.

I am so privileged to serve with OMS as a missionary. Because of my work here, I have had many opportunities to grow in my search for persons of peace. I am working to facilitate house-church planting movements in different regions of Asia. Training and encouraging national Christians to search for persons of peace, and then to carry out evangelism, discipleship, and church planting, is one of the most fulfilling and rewarding ministries I have ever been a part of. I also train newly appointed OMS missionaries in these same subjects as preparation before going to their fields of service. The Lord gave me a call to a particular population several years ago, and when I am not training others, I am searching for persons of peace among women who are trafficked or trapped in the sex-industry businesses such as strip clubs. I train Christian women to form teams to help in this work named Light in Darkness Ministry.

In the following chapters, you will learn about the three characteristics of persons of peace: they are receptive, they are well-known and have a reputation, and they are connected with others and refer them to the messengers of the good news of Jesus. I will be relating stories about biblical personalities, historical examples, and present-day witnesses who have a divine appointment with persons of peace. Because of my love of OMS, you will be reading many examples from its ministries in these chapters. I hope you enjoy the journey as we examine what it means to be a person of peace.

Chapter 3

A Person of Peace Is Receptive

A person who is receptive is one who is willing to receive something. When people are receptive, they have an open mind and are willing to listen to a new idea or suggestion. They are welcoming to the one who is offering to share an item or information. Therefore, persons of peace are willing to listen to God's witnesses who come to give them a testimony or message from the Lord. Their hearts and minds are open to the Holy Spirit and to the truths in God's Word. Persons of peace may not immediately seek the Lord or pray the first time we encounter them; however, the door is left open for further conversations. They are interested in the Lord and desire to hear more.

Through the following stories, we will learn about persons of peace who appear in the Bible, who were historical pioneer missionaries, and many who are present-day witnesses. We will see that prayer plays an important role in paving the way for people to open their hearts to the Lord. Sometimes the conversion takes more than one witness and is a long process, but we will see how God is orchestrating behind the scenes to prepare hearts to receive his message of salvation and to bring other people across the paths of his messengers. We also celebrate that God is willing to go to great miraculous lengths in order to reach a person of peace.

Biblical Characters

Aeneas of Lydda

In Acts 9:32-35, we learn about a receptive person of peace named Aeneas. Aeneas lived in Lydda, a lovely town about eleven miles southeast of Joppa and halfway between Jerusalem and the coast of the Mediterranean Sea. Lydda was on a fertile plain and had good grazing land. Lydda was not large, so most people either knew each other or were familiar with family names.

At the beginning of his story, Aeneas had been paralyzed and bedridden for eight years. By that time, his muscles had deteriorated completely. Life for Aeneas was filled with drudgery, difficulty, and boredom. His instinct to provide for and protect his family was thwarted, and now he was the weak one. His self-esteem and identity as a man must have suffered, and he surely endured periods of depression and grief. Most paralytics did not survive long in the first century, so Aeneas must have had a wonderful family who gave him the best of care to enable him to survive for eight years.

One day, Peter was traveling across the country to visit the followers of Christ in Lydda, and he encountered Aeneas. Peter immediately told him that Jesus Christ was healing him. Peter then instructed Aeneas to get up and roll up his sleeping mat. Jesus healed Aeneas instantly. His paralysis was not only gone, but his muscles had also returned to normal size and vitality because he could immediately walk.

And walk he did. He was so happy that he walked all over the town so that each person could see him healed. Aeneas's healing had such a powerful effect on the town of Lydda that all who saw him turned to the Lord. His healing testimony connected Aeneas as a person of peace to the broader community of Lydda, and he became a bridge to their salvation.

Aeneas did not have to hear the message more than once

to believe it with his whole heart. He was a completely receptive person of peace and ready to receive all the good news that God had for him in his life. Not only does Aeneas exhibit the quality of receptivity, he also encompasses the other two qualities as well. Through the testimony of his healing, Aeneas referred an entire town to our Redeemer, and his reputation grew throughout the community so that he could impact the eternal destinies of the townspeople.

This story should encourage us as witnesses because it illustrates that nothing is too difficult for God, even healing seriously ill people. Whenever we enter a home in search of a person of peace and with the hope of sharing the Gospel, we need to be as faithful as Peter in praying for the sick ones who may be in that home. Jesus commands us to care for the sick and to tell them that 'the kingdom of God has come near you' (Luke 10:9).

We never know when God has a miracle in mind for a person of peace in answer to one of our prayers. It is easy to pray for a person with a bad cold or a sore throat, but our faith may be stretched when we are confronted with someone like Aeneas, who is paralyzed, or someone who is blind or suffering from a terminal disease. Would this situation stretch you? Do you believe that you can lay hands on the sick and pray for them as you go out as a witness?

Take the step of faith and obedience and pray for those who are sick. God may use you in ways you never dreamed possible, and he may be preparing the way for another receptive person of peace through that healing testimony.

The Jailer of Philippi

In Acts 16, we learn an incredible story about the jailer of Paul and Silas. These two men were in Philippi to pray with new believers when they encountered a slave girl who was possessed by a spirit that enabled her to predict the future. She made lots of money as a fortune-teller for her masters. Being troubled by the girl's prophesying, Paul commanded the evil spirit to come out of her in the name of Jesus. When that happened, and because the girl could no longer see the future, her owners lost all the income that she had been making for them. In their anger, they dragged Paul and Silas before the town magistrates, who ordered them stripped, beaten, and thrown into prison.

The magistrates told the jailer to guard the prisoners carefully, so the jailer put Paul and Silas into an inner cell and clamped their feet in the stocks. Their imprisonment did not stop the two men from witnessing through prayer and song to the other prisoners, who listened to them. At midnight, a powerful earthquake occurred, and the prison was shaken so badly that the doors flew open and all the chains came loose.

The jailer came running and believed that the prisoners had escaped. He was about to kill himself in fear when Paul yelled for him to stop and assured him that all the prisoners were still there. The jailer was amazed at what had happened and immediately begged to be saved. Although the jailer worked day and night with hardened criminals and should have been cynical and disbelieving, God knew his heart and brought Paul and Silas to him at exactly the right moment.

The jailer was a receptive person of peace and knew the truth when he heard it for the first time from Paul and Silas. To the jailer, these two men were different from all the other people that the jailer knew. After listening to Paul and Silas in the prison cell, the jailer also knew that God had confirmed their words with this miraculous earthquake. That very night, he received Christ. The jailer became the bridge of faith to his family so that his entire household was not only saved, but baptized as well.

We can learn a lesson from this story about the jailer. When we interact with new believers, we should teach them not only biblical truths, but we should also consider ways to help them become a bridge to other people among their families, friends, and workplaces. We must target all the connections that new believers have in their communities. The church needs to understand the meaning of the term *person of peace* as we look for receptive people.

The example lived out by Paul and Silas is so inspirational. Instead of being angry at their imprisonment, they were singing and praising God and teaching the other prisoners about Christ. Could you have this attitude after being persecuted by ungodly people? As witnesses in search of persons of peace, we too can expect suffering and attacks orchestrated by the Enemy of our souls. Are you prepared to persevere?

The Lame Man of Jerusalem

In Acts 3, we are introduced to a receptive man who was lame from birth. To survive, he begged daily at the temple gate in Jerusalem. His life was without dignity. One day, at about three in the afternoon, Peter and John were going up to the temple to pray. When they encountered the lame man at the gate, he started to beg for money.

Peter looked at the man intently, trying to determine the state of the man's heart. In response to what Peter saw, Peter told the lame man that he didn't have money, but he would give him what he did have, which was the power to heal. So in the name of Jesus, Peter commanded the man to walk.

Instantly, the man's feet straightened out and became completely normal and strong. He could feel the blood rushing in and his bones actually growing. Not only did he walk, as Peter commanded, but he also jumped and praised God in the temple courts, his first act as a new Christian. He was receptive from the very first time that he heard Peter speak. God knew his heart was ready – aching even – to believe.

Not only did this miracle impact the life of the lame man, but it also impacted the lives of hundreds of people who saw the miracle in the temple courts and knew the lame man from his vigils at the gate. The healing created an opportunity for a Gospel stream to begin to flow and to connect Peter to many more people. Peter was able to share a message with the growing crowd, and many more believed. Before Peter and John were arrested by the temple guards at the urging of the priests and Sadducees, they converted nearly five thousand people. This success was the direct result of one receptive person of peace.

Many times, a person with a tiny grain of faith may be on the verge of a much greater belief. What that person needs to see is the power of the Lord manifested somehow in his own life or in the life of a loved one. Therefore, Jesus commands us to go in his name and in his authority to perform miracles, signs, and wonders. We too are to cast out demons and to pray for the sick to be healed. Is your faith strong enough to obey the promptings of the Holy Spirit and to ask God to show his great power?

Cornelius of Caesarea

In Acts 10, we meet Cornelius, a God-fearing Roman who lived in Caesarea, a town on the coast of the Mediterranean Sea, a little over thirty miles north of Joppa. Caesarea was the most important port city in Judea and was the capital of this Roman province. It was a bustling city with travelers coming and going by sea and by roads from every direction.

The Romans naturally had a military presence in Caesarea, and Cornelius was a powerful centurion – the commander of 100 soldiers – in charge of the Italian regiment. He was, ironically, a receptive person of peace in the army ranks. Unlike other Roman soldiers who were steeped in the worship of their many gods, Cornelius prayed regularly to the one true God. He was also involved in many good works, including being generous to the poor. But he was a Gentile in the eyes of the Jews of the day.

The Lord knew Cornelius's desire for truth and righteousness, so one day Cornelius received a vision from God. The vision was that of an angel who told him that his prayers and gifts had been received by the Lord as an offering. He was then told to send men to Joppa to bring back Simon Peter. Cornelius did not delay. He was immediately receptive to God's command, and he sent servants as soon as the vision ended.

At this same time, Peter was praying on the roof of the house where he was staying in Joppa. Suddenly, he was seeing a vision too. In that vision, a voice was telling him to eat unclean animals. This vision was repulsive to Peter because it went against all the teachings he had heard his entire Jewish life. But the voice spoke to Peter again and said, *"What God has cleansed you must not call common"* (Acts 10:15).

Peter was trying to figure out what God wanted him to do about the vision when Cornelius's servants approached the house in perfect accord with God's timing. Peter would soon realize that the vision was not just about food; it was about people too. Because all other ethnic groups were considered unclean by the Jews, God was talking about cleaning up Gentiles and allowing them to be a part of his kingdom.

The idea of opening up the kingdom to Gentiles was an important principle under the new covenant. It was a principle that would ultimately change the world. The new Christian church in Jerusalem was about to be rocked with this truth. So just to make sure that Peter really did understand the concept, the Lord gave him the same vision three times.

By the end of the third vision, the servants of Cornelius had arrived. The Lord told Peter to go with these men immediately. God was taking no chances that this encounter could be thwarted. Peter was beginning to understand the vision now, and when he arrived in Caesarea, he shared his vision with Cornelius and told him that God did not show favoritism and that God accepted people from every nation who wanted to serve and obey him. What a remarkable step that was for Peter and for the new Christian church.

Then Peter began to tell Cornelius and all the people he had gathered together about Jesus, God's Son. The truth about Jesus was the message that God longed for these Gentiles to know. In the house of Cornelius, Peter gave one of the most beautiful and succinct presentations of the Gospel that is recorded in all of the New Testament. And he gave it to a Gentile – a hated Roman officer – and his family.

Cornelius and his household accepted and believed in Jesus as Peter was speaking. Before the preaching was over, the Holy Spirit was being poured out on the Gentiles in amazing ways. People began to shout out praises to God as others started speaking in tongues. They believed. They all were born again. Peter finally understood: Jesus came for the whole world, not just for the Jews.

Talk about a receptive audience. Peter wasn't even finished speaking, and the Holy Spirit was busy saving these people, one after another. Even today, God has receptive people whose hearts are ready for the message that you will bring them. Exciting adventures await you in searching for persons of peace. Will you trust God and go when and where he calls you on a mission?

Cornelius was rich; Peter was poor. Cornelius was well educated; Peter was a common laborer. Cornelius was a Gentile and a citizen of the most powerful ruling nation of the known world; Peter was a Jew and under the control of Rome. Peter had been brought up with hatred for the Romans, but God changed his heart and gave him love and acceptance for Cornelius. The Lord will also give you love for those to whom he calls you to witness, no matter how different you are from them.

The Lord does not show favoritism. His heart is equally broken by the wealthy businessman in his corner office on Wall Street, the pre-teen girl cutting herself in her bedroom in England, or the Samburu tribesman watching his goats in Kenya. The Lord's message of salvation is for all people, from every tribe and nation. All God needs now is for people to be just like Peter, willing to go.

Historical Pioneer Missionaries

Child of a Slave

In 1722, Count Nikolaus Ludwig von Zinzendorf opened up part of his estate in Herrnhut, Germany, to several hundred persecuted believers, who came mostly from the Kingdom of Bohemia and from Moravia. After the Reformation, thousands of these new Protestants had been forced to flee for their lives from persecution because they were branded as heretics. The Count helped them to build one of the first Christian communes, where they called themselves Moravians. Their main priorities included seeking God in prayer, searching for spiritual growth and accountability, and having unity in the body of Christ.

One day, the Count brought a special guest to the Moravians' community. He brought a former slave named Anton Ulrich. Ulrich told the group how he had been captured as a youth from his country in West Africa. He had been chained, sold in a market, placed on a ship with many others, and taken to a large plantation. There he was branded and housed like an animal. His captors gave him a new name and forbade him from using his real name. His family, home, and identity were lost to him forever.

Ulrich told the group that he had obtained his freedom and shared his thankfulness to God for salvation. Then he told them of his great burden for the other slaves to hear the good news. He shared with them that he had a sister, named Anna, who was still on the island. While he walked as a free man, he could hardly bear the knowledge that his sister was still suffering in slavery and did not have the assurance of eternal life. He begged the Moravians to send people to this island to bring the slaves the message of salvation.

The Moravians were filled with compassion, but they were troubled at the same time because no Protestant missionaries existed up to this point. Most of them had been trying to begin new lives in Germany without constant threats to their safety. However, several young Moravian men spent time with Ulrich and asked more questions. The Holy Spirit began to speak to a few, and they began to dream of the possibility of going to the slaves as missionaries.

Eventually, the commune sent two men – Leonard Dober and David Nitschmann – to the West Indies to minister to the slaves. They moved onto an island and lived among the island population. They lived much as the slaves did to lessen the barriers and to have opportunities to speak to them about Jesus in their limited time after work. The slaves were suspicious at first, and some were openly hostile.

Leonard became discouraged until he met a young boy who was the child of a slave. This young boy believed that Leonard wanted to be his friend and was a man who told the truth. Over several months, Leonard shared Jesus with the youngster when no one else wanted to listen.

One day, the boy prayed to receive Jesus. He was the first receptive listener on the island, and he gave the missionaries the hope and strength to continue their work. Not only was the boy receptive, but he also referred the missionaries to all of his family and neighbors, and he helped open doors to new contacts that had been closed for years. Over time, more slaves converted to Christianity on the island, and the Moravians sent more missionaries to help in the work. Eventually, the Moravians found Ulrich's sister, Anna, and she received Jesus too.

The courage of these two young Moravian men created a phenomenal missionary movement: the birth of the first Protestant church to grasp the missionary purpose of the church. The Moravian missionary movement proved the effectiveness of world missions and convinced doubters that the "heathen could be saved." The Moravians grasped the truth that the prime obligation of the church is evangelism and that every member of the Christian church has this responsibility. They also understood an important part of the search for persons of peace: the effort must be bathed in prayer. The Moravians at Herrnhut started a twenty-four-hour-a-day prayer chain that remained unending for more than 100 years.

Satan probably laughed at Leonard when his only convert was a child, and he probably tried to make his efforts seem worthless. Has Satan ever attacked you in this way? Has he ever made you feel that your work in the kingdom is not having any effect and that you are wasting your time? Be encouraged by the experience of Leonard Dober and David Nitschmann. Our entire world was.

Ko Tha Byu

In 1817, Adoniram Judson disembarked from a ship near Rangoon, Burma, after a long and difficult journey from America. He came with a Bible, of course, as all missionaries did; however, he did not yet understand the impact that his arrival with that book would make on millions of receptive persons of peace living within a distance of a few hundred miles.

Judson found lodging and soon began the task of learning the language. As soon as he could, he ventured out into the marketplaces and preached the Gospel to the Buddhists. Sadly, he got very little response from them. Judson preached for seven years with no success, and he struggled with depression and discouragement. To give himself something to do during this time, Judson translated the Bible into Burmese. God would ultimately bless this endeavor because this Burmese Bible would soon become the foundation for many missionaries to use in the future.

Unknown to Judson, members of the Karen people, an ethnic group living in Burma, were daily passing by his home during those seven years. The Karen people believed in Y'we, the one true God, and they were a receptive people just waiting to be found. One day God sent Ko Tha Byu, a member of the Karen people, to Judson's home to look for work. Judson gave him some jobs to do, but wondered if he had made a mistake because Ko Tha Byu had such a violent temper. Ko Tha Byu told Judson that he had killed thirty men.

Despite Ko Tha Byu's temper, Judson shared the Gospel with him as often as possible. At first, the man didn't understand what Judson was telling him. Then one day all the pieces of the puzzle came together, and Ko Tha Byu began to ask questions about the "white strangers" who had brought the message and about the book that contained the message. Ko Tha Byu grew more and more excited, and soon he gladly accepted the gift of salvation through Jesus Christ, our Lord. Overnight, he became the most eager disciple Judson could have asked for, a true receptive person of peace.

During those days, two more missionaries, George and Sarah Boardman, arrived in Burma to open a training school for new converts. Ko Tha Byu had never dreamed of attending school, but he happily enrolled. He was filled with an urgency for learning how to read the Bible, and he was totally preoccupied with studying. He had a great aptitude for learning God's Word.

To help the missionaries understand why learning about the Bible was so important, Ko Tha Byu explained the spiritual history of his people and how they had lost the knowledge of God. He told the missionaries that his people had been waiting to receive the Lost Book for centuries. They used to know Y'we, the one true God, but they had sinned, and the knowledge of him was lost to his people. They were separated from Y'we through their rebellion, and they did not know the way back to him. However, one of their prophets told them that white-skinned strangers would one day bring a book that would explain the message of truth and would establish a relationship with Y'we once again.

The missionaries were speechless. The Bible that Judson had been translating all those years when he thought he was accomplishing nothing was the very book that brought Ko Tha Byu to his belief in Christ and made him a receptive person of peace. It was the very book that Ko Tha Byu felt he had to learn to read so that he could take its message to his people as soon as he could. The prophecy of the Lost Book had been fulfilled at last.

Ko Tha Byu was soon baptized and left with the Boardmans to begin his work near the Karen people. Day after day, he went into the hills and found villages of Karen people. Each time he preached the good news, nearly every person in the village would respond with wonder. Hundreds would then come flocking to see the white people who had brought them the Lost Book. Ko Tha Byu climbed high hills and crossed rivers; he traveled during the monsoon season; he tirelessly took the message to one village after another. After Ko Tha Byu proclaimed his message in the villages, George Boardman was then invited to supplement that teaching with more lessons from the Lost Book. The Karen people were eager students and their hearts were completely receptive to all the teachings of the Word.

Ko Tha Byu is known as the Karen Apostle in many mission societies today and is an example of a receptive person of peace. When we first met him, he was an unlikely candidate to be a minister of the Gospel because of his violent temper and past. He was also a poor man of no reputation when he first believed. But the Lord saw a person of peace in Ko Tha Byu and turned him into a man of great reputation and influence. The Lord knew the exact time that Ko Tha Byu's heart was ready to receive and recognize the truth, so when the Burmese Bible was ready, the Lord brought Ko Tha Byu to Judson to hear the Gospel. The Lord also knew that Ko Tha Byu was a man of spirit and determination who could travel and preach the Word to his people. His receptive heart triggered one of the greatest revivals to a people group in all of mission history.

Just as the Lord did for Ko Tha Byu, the Lord can turn any person with a passion for evil into a person with a passion for good. Do you know someone who may be receptive to God's Word but who has a reputation for violence or uncontrollable behavior? Have you let their actions deter you from approaching them with the Gospel message? Try to reach out to these people anyway. You just may be surprised too.

Men of the Lahu Tribe

In 1887, a young man from Nebraska named William Marcus Young made his way to an uncharted and isolated area of Burma called the Shan State. He went in answer to a call from God that placed an overwhelming burden on his heart to bring thousands of souls to the Lord. Young knew that he was under God's authority, so he prayed every day for God to bring people that needed to know the Lord to him. He prayed while traveling from village to village. He prayed himself to sleep every night, and he prayed every morning when he awoke at dawn. Many long and lonely years of hardship and disappointment went by, and he saw little response to the Gospel message.

But God heard each prayer that Young uttered, and the Lord

was putting a plan in motion to answer those prayers. One day, Young was preaching in an open-air village to the Shan people. He was wearing the light-colored clothes that most westerners wore at that time. He had his Bible open, and the white pages were bright in the sunlight. His white face was gleaming from sweat from the heat of the day. Young was preaching about the Ten Commandments of Moses. He was explaining about the laws of the one true God when he began to notice some strangely clothed men coming toward him out of the crowd. They were not Shan tribesmen.

Young learned that these men were from the Lahu tribe who lived on some distant mountains. The Lahu people, much like the Karen people of Rangoon, Burma, had a prophecy given to them long ago about a white man who would bring them a white book that contained the truth about Gwi'sha, the one true God. The men wore bracelets of coarse rope around their wrists. These ropes symbolized the bondage they were in to evil spirits. Only the true messenger of Gwi'sha would be able to cut off the ropes and free them from bondage.

These men completely surrounded Young and stared at him in amazement. They listened intently to his message while they stared at the white pages of the Bible in his hands. Suddenly, the Lahu men could contain themselves no longer. With powerful emotion, they pleaded with Young to come with them right away. They told him that they had been waiting for him for centuries and that they had already built meeting houses for him to use to speak to the villagers. They asked Young to come to their villages and to bring the white book of Gwi'sha to their homes. Receptive persons of peace were right before his eyes.

Young and several other missionaries traveled with these persons of peace back to their homes in the mountains. As they went from Lahu village to Lahu village, literally tens of thousands of people received the Savior. In the annals of mission history, this story is similar to something you might read in the book of Acts. So many requests for teaching came in that the missionaries could not get to all the places. The Lahu villagers experienced many happy ceremonies to cut off the ropes of bondage to evil spirits. After these ceremonies, the people were baptized.

Young understood the concept of equipping the new converts to build bridges among their own people, so the missionaries began schools to train the Lahu to teach their own people about the Lord. Young even recruited his young sons, Harold and Vincent, to begin to travel and preach at a young age because additional teachers were so needed. For many decades, the missionaries recorded that approximately two thousand people per year were baptized.

God knew the hearts of the Lahu people were ready to receive the truth. He knew that they longed to be released from the bondage of the evil spirits, so he prepared the way through prophetic messages in their culture and through the presence of William Marcus Young. God knew he could trust Young with this mission because he was a man of prayer and was faithful in preaching the truth. So God graciously sent him not one receptive person of peace, but tens of thousands. The legacy of the Young family continues even today as his grandsons and great-grandsons continue to serve God around the world.

How would you describe your burden for the lost? Do you pray for lost souls every day? Do you beg God to allow you to lead people to Christ? Will you begin to pray for God to send you persons of peace? God will give you the desires of your heart just as he did for William Marcus Young.

Women of India

"Amy, you can't do that. It's just not done." the missionary women told her emphatically.

Amy Carmichael was wearing a sari, the traditional dress of Indian women. A sari is made of yards and yards of draping fabric. Saris come in every color and are often decorated with embroidery, beads, or sequins. Wealthy women wear saris made from pure silk. The cheapest sari, worn by the poorest women, is made of plain white cotton. Carmichael was wearing one of the white cotton saris.

Amy Carmichael moved to Pannaivilai, India, in 1895, from Ireland, and had been working hard to learn the language. She felt confused at the ladies' outburst because she had worn a kimono in Japan to break down barriers with the women there. She didn't understand how her dress could be such a big deal. The difference was that India was under British rule, and the British were supposed to demonstrate that all things British were superior to anything Indian.

Although living far away from the motherland, the British – including the missionaries – strove to preserve every custom and manner proudly, and no true British subject would wear a sari in public.

Carmichael ignored the comments of the missionary women and decided to wear the sari. Her purpose was to find persons of peace and lead them to Jesus. Carmichael did not want to flaunt that she was a member of any ruling country. She was already different in her language, geographical background, and beliefs. She didn't want any other barrier to her friendship and communication with Indian women.

Carmichael's dream as a pioneer missionary was to find women who were receptive to the Gospel, train them in evangelism, and then travel together from village to village sharing the Gospel. This dream was unheard of in its day. Indian women didn't travel. Most of them were married by the time they were fifteen or sixteen, and their husbands had complete control over them. The women had to work from morning till night tending fires, carrying water, rearing children, preparing food, washing clothes, and cleaning their homes. They had no time for travel and evangelism.

The British missionaries viewed Carmichael as a young, unrealistic female at best, or a disruptive team member at worst. The only thing Carmichael knew to do in the face of their disapproval was to pray, so she prayed fervently for Indian women who were receptive to the Gospel and who would be able to do evangelistic ministry with her.

One day, the Lord led her to Ponnamel, a young widow under the care of her father-in-law. Since her husband's death, she had been forced to become a servant in his household because widows were still considered to be the property of the husband's family after death. Ponnamel became Amy's friend and disciple, a receptive person of peace. The family did attend church, but her father-in-law still kept idols and didn't believe in breaking caste.

As Ponnamel grew in her faith, her church allowed her to teach Sunday school, and she was good at it. Using Ponnamel's gift of teaching as an excuse, Carmichael went to the pastor and told him her dream about taking Ponnamel with her on evangelism trips. She convinced the pastor to speak with Ponnamel's father-in-law for her release from his house. With the Lord's help, the pastor convinced the old man to release Ponnamel.

Ponnamel and Carmichael became a powerful team. They used a unique method to share the Word: After they arrived at a village in the morning, they headed toward the market where they found a shady place to sit and pray. They prayed for God to send receptive persons of peace right to their shady place. They also asked permission from the village elders to preach in the open air in the evenings. The Lord answered these prayers and brought many souls into the kingdom one by one.

The Lord didn't stop with Ponnamel in answering Carmichael's prayers. He sent her another receptive person of peace. This woman, named Sellamutthu, had lost an arm. She became a lovely Christian, and her family willingly let her go because they thought that no one would ever want her in marriage. They also saw her as a financial burden. But both the Lord and Carmichael saw Sellamutthu as a huge blessing. She joyfully endured the trials of travel and readily shared with the villagers about the mercy and love of the Lord in her life.

God even stirred the heart of a married woman named Marial. At the beginning, even Carmichael didn't believe that Marial's husband would allow her to do evangelism. But the husband became a believer too. Not only did he allow Marial to travel with Carmichael and evangelize, but he also offered to be the cook on their journeys. The Lord successfully introduced Carmichael to two receptive persons of peace. Marial became a powerful witness, and the nourishment prepared by her husband sustained the team day by day.

Just as God answered Amy Carmichael's prayers for receptive persons of peace, he will surely answer yours. Carmichael prayed that her persons of peace would become evangelists with her, and that request also reflects the heart of God. From the beginning, Carmichael's goal with a new believer was to train that person for ministry and to partner with her in bringing in a harvest of souls. It is not God's will that any person should perish. When we pray for persons of peace, we can have confidence in entering God's throne room because we are praying according to his will.

Do you have a plan to find and train persons of peace? People gave Amy all kinds of excuses as to why her plan would not work. They tried to put doubt in her mind that her idea would succeed. Perhaps you too have had a dream for ministry. If God has birthed an idea in your heart and given you a burden for a particular place or people, don't let anyone stand in your way.

Juan Ayllon

Juan Ayllon was born in 1917 in the village of Pelechuco, Bolivia, which is located near the peaks of the Andes Mountains. He was of mixed heritage, half-Bolivian-Indian and half-Mestizo. Ayllon was only two years old when he became ill. Because he cried and was fretful, his father threw urine into the little boy's eyes and made him almost completely blind. His mother took him to one person after another for help and advice, but he ultimately faced the world with this hardship.

Ayllon's first contact with the Gospel came when he was a young boy. Ayllon was walking down the street when a stranger handed him some Gospel tracts. He read them over and was fascinated by the life that was described in those tracts. The words fell on fertile soil, and his heart was receptive to the truth. But one of his friends at school tore up the tracts and told him they were of the Devil, so Ayllon had no other contact with Christians for many years.

At the age of nineteen, Juan Ayllon got a job working for the railroad, where he met the second Christian to come into his life. One day, men at the railroad were stealing sweets from a little boy who had come there to sell them. The boy cried because he had no money to take home to his family. As Ayllon watched, a fellow worker went over to the boy, put his arm around him, and spoke comfortingly to the child. Then the worker did something surprising: he lovingly repaid all the money that was stolen. This kind action made Ayllon curious, and he asked the man why he gave the child the money.

The man answered with his personal testimony. He shared how Jesus had changed his life and how he now wanted to be kind to others. Then he invited Ayllon to his church, became his friend, and began to help him understand the Bible. Ayllon became a Christian through this man's loving outreach. He was receptive to that man's Christian witness because he saw him do an act of selfless love.

Before long, Ayllon was a faithful member of the church, and he was the happiest he had ever been. Only one problem remained: his mother was a devout Roman Catholic, and she reacted harshly to her son's conversion. She believed that Ayllon had betrayed her, and she turned on him with hatred and derision. Sometimes she even called him the son of Satan. Ayllon patiently demonstrated love in return, just as he had been taught by his mentor. Through his faithful testimony, Ayllon eventually led his mother to receive Christ as her Savior.

God continued to bring others into Ayllon's life to teach and inspire him. He joined a team that did evangelism outreach in the plazas, and he handed out tracts like the ones that had captured his heart as a young boy. Then Ayllon heard of a Bible school in Guatemala, and he felt called to go; however, he had no money and no way to get there. He prayed about his situation and felt that God was telling him to go to this school, so he sold all of his possessions and journeyed to Guatemala.

Ayllon encountered many adventures on his way to Guatemala, including being forced into slavery aboard a ship by a ruthless captain. Ayllon managed to escape off the coast of New York City, where he was befriended by several Christians who provided him with funds to safely reach his destination. A journey of a few days ended up taking 104 days. But God was always at work with a plan for Ayllon. At long last, Ayllon reached the Bible school. He was five months late, but the people greeted him with love and friendship.

Ayllon proved to be a brilliant student and was soon working as a teacher's assistant. He spent his time after school doing evangelism in local towns and villages. The fire birthed in him by his Christian witnesses burned brightly all his life. He established many churches during his lifetime, including one of the largest churches in La Paz, Bolivia. Ayllon's crowning achievement was his eventual employment by the American Bible Society, where, despite his poor eyesight, he translated the Bible into the Aymara language, one of the oldest languages on the South American continent.

God used several witnesses in simple ways to reach Ayllon, a great example of a receptive person of peace. His receptive heart was first touched by a witness giving out Gospel tracts when he was a child. His heart was then changed by a witness who showed an act of love to a poor, helpless boy who had been robbed. His heart was inspired to do evangelism by church friends who took the time to disciple and equip him to do ministry. Finally, he was rescued from slavery and sent on his way to school through the generosity of more of God's witnesses who were in the right place at the right time. Then God used Ayllon to connect thousands of people to the Gospel message through his translation work.

How is God using you? Are you sowing seeds in search of persons of peace? Are seekers drawn to you through your acts of lovingkindness? Are you pouring your life into a new person of peace to help that person grow? Are you sharing your blessings so that others can be trained and equipped to do evangelism? We are all needed as links in a chain in God's kingdom. He needs to use us all in his plans for reaching one soul after another. Make sure you're not a missing link.

Chi-oang

Jim and Lillian Dickson went to Formosa as pioneer missionaries in 1927. Formosa, now called Taiwan, is an island off of mainland China. The island is around 250 miles long and 50 miles wide in most places. The terrain has great variety with fertile plains on the western side and high mountains on the central and eastern parts. The climate is warm, and many species of fruits and flowers bloom all year-round. The people grow an abundance of sugar cane and rice, the food staple of Asia.

In 1927, six million Chinese lived on Formosa along with five hundred thousand Japanese who ruled the island. In addition to the Chinese and Japanese people, several tribes of aboriginal mountain people, numbering close to two hundred thousand, also lived on the island at that time. They continued to live the way their ancestors had lived hundreds of years before. One of these aboriginal groups was the Tyal tribe. These people were aggressive headhunters who lived in inaccessible areas high in the mountains. The Dicksons had been burdened for the people of the Tyal tribe from the beginning of their move to Formosa, but the Japanese made it difficult to get to them.

After one of Jim Dickson's pioneering trips into the mountains, he brought back a woman who looked utterly bizarre. She walked twenty feet behind Dickson as he approached his home. His wife's first reaction was, "*What* is that?" Barbaric seemed to be the best description. All across her face, from ear to ear, were tattoos that made her look fierce and threatening. But Dickson reassured his wife by telling her that Chi-oang was the first Christian believer in the Tyal tribe and the first receptive person of peace among the headhunters. She had responded to Jim's message in an outdoor meeting and received Jesus as her Savior.

Dickson's plan for Chi-oang was to put her in Bible school to prepare her to go back to her people. With a spirit of determination, Chi-oang worked so hard over the following months that she actually led the entire Bible school. When she completed her education, she said her good-byes, and everyone prayed for her safe return to her people and for her success in spreading the Gospel message. The Dicksons knew they might never see Chi-oang again.

Soon after Chi-oang returned to her people, the Japanese

began to interfere with the ministry because they objected to any outreach to the mountain tribes. They would not let the aborigines come off the mountains, and they would not let the missionaries go up into the mountains to do ministry. The Japanese made it illegal to give the aborigines Bibles, but the missionaries managed to smuggle some in to the people. One day, a Japanese policeman found a Bible in a Tyal home. The Japanese brought in more police to search all the Tyal houses for Bibles. The police burned any Bibles that they found and brought in the Tyal owners for questioning. The persecution of the Tyal people had begun.

Many years went by before the Dicksons had any word from Chi-oang. When it finally came, it was in the form of a postcard that read: "The Tyals have been beaten until the blood came because they believed in Christ." The Dicksons were heartbroken. They felt powerless to help, and feared the Tyal people would never keep the faith when met with such persecution while still babes in Christ. However, they did not know the rest of the story. They later learned that after the beatings, the Tyal had bravely told the police that they would remain Christians even if they were beaten to death.

Communication was nearly impossible, but the Dicksons did not give up praying for the work of Chi-oang. More years passed before they discovered that Chi-oang had been teaching all over the mountains. And when she could no longer travel the mountain trails, people traveled to her. She faithfully taught the message of the Gospel to as many people as she could reach. The Japanese had tried to kill her again and again, but men guarded her as they would a great treasure. They had even carried her to safety several times when she was too feeble to walk.

When missionaries finally had the freedom to go up the mountains, they found entire villages converted to Christ. They found churches built right in the middle of the villages, the most important place of honor. The missionaries would always ask, "Who brought you the good news of Jesus?" And the answer always was: "Chi-oang told us of the one true God and the Savior, Jesus, who was sent." The Formosan Christians began to call this wonder *The Pentecost of the Hills*. At that time, four thousand believers existed in the Tyal tribe, and two thousand credited their salvation to Chi-oang.

As the Tyal people began to venture down the mountains, they would go to the Formosan Christian churches with eagerness and joy, and they would go to the believers' homes as well. They had a great thirst for knowledge and wanted to learn the Bible better. They wanted to be sure that they were worshiping correctly, because they had only one Bible from which to learn.

The Dicksons dealt with conditions in Formosa that included extreme forms of paganism, filth, and sordidness. Outsiders often asked them how they could continue to minister to men and women in such extreme darkness. But their response was always an affirmation of love and devotion to Christ because they knew God needed to use them to discover persons of peace. They focused on the potential of lives that could be made to give God glory, and they dreamed of the people beyond them that the persons of peace would reach.

Persons of peace have the potential to reach generations through their children, grandchildren, great-grandchildren, friends, and neighbors who can then influence their own families. The possibilities are endless for a long chain of new names to be written in the Book of Life because of one person of peace. We must always look beyond what we can see in the physical world and minister by faith in the spiritual realm. May we have our Father's eyes to see the bigger picture of hope and salvation.

Present-Day Witnesses

Man on the Train

"What is that song you are singing? It is beautiful!" the man on the train exclaimed. This was the opening question in a divine appointment between strangers on a miserably hot and crowded train in rural India.

Anil's joy always bubbled over as he talked with people about Jesus and how he was planting house churches in the surrounding area. Anil had joined Every Community for Christ two years earlier as a trainer, and he had already begun training more than a dozen men and women to start and lead house churches in a small village in northern India.

Looking at Samita, one would expect this young Indian woman with downcast eyes to be shy and quiet. With her carefully wrapped red sari, her oiled hair in a long black braid, her dainty steps, and her constant deference to others, what else would one think? However, behind that mild exterior is a passionate young woman who is always willing to tell others what she believes.

In Indian culture, families arrange marriages for their children, but Samita decided it was time to help her family in the selection process. Samita was bold when she approached her parents and told them that she really liked Anil and how he shared his Christian faith in her village. Samita's parents were agreeable to the match, and after conversations with Anil's parents, they discovered that Anil liked Samita as well. Plans moved quickly, and within weeks, they were married. Samita moved into Anil's simple baked-brick home.

Anil began immediately to train Samita to do ministry with him. Samita prayed with power and treated many suffering women in their community with tender compassion. She soon began to travel with Anil to visit his disciples and their house churches. During these visits, Anil preached to the men, women, and children about Jesus, while Samita would teach them praise songs in Hindi and lead the women in prayer.

Only two months after their wedding, Anil and Samita were coming home from just such a visit when they encountered the man on the train. Trains are always crowded in India, so they squeezed into a seat with three others, with five others sitting across from them, knees touching knees. Anil wanted to help his wife with the praise songs she had been singing, so he began to sing softly so as not to bother anyone else.

Just then, a man enthusiastically asked about the song. Startled, but pleased, Anil seized the moment and began to explain that the song was praising Jesus Christ. Soon Samita and Anil found themselves singing more songs for the man and all who wanted to listen in their compartment. At their journey's end, the man discovered that Anil and Samita lived only three kilometers from his home, so he invited them to come and tell his family more about Jesus. They exchanged phone numbers, and Anil promised that he and Samita would visit the man's home.

The next day, Anil and Samita were resting from their long trip when the phone rang. It was the man from the train. He wanted them to come to his home soon because his family was eager to hear about Jesus. Anil promised they would come the next day and arranged a time to meet. He and Samita prayed that hearts would be ready to believe that night, and they prayed again in the morning.

As they entered the man's village, he was waiting on the road. He enthusiastically welcomed Anil and Samita to his village and thanked them for coming. As they walked to the house, the man saw an old woman sitting by the road, so he invited her to come to his home. She slowly stood, arranged her sari, and followed. Then they passed some men working in a field. The man also pleaded with them to take a break from their work to come to his house. They put down their tools and also followed. God answered the prayers of Anil and Samita that day. They stayed for hours, sharing about Jesus and singing praise songs. The Spirit came upon Anil, and he danced and sang with enthusiasm. His eyes shown with excitement and the joy of the Lord. Everyone in the man's household confessed their faith in Jesus, and a new house church was born that very day.

God is at work connecting witnesses of his grace and salvation with persons of peace who are ready to receive the message. This person of peace immediately reached out to his family and community with the good news he had heard. A Greek professor once said that the Great Commission, found in Matthew 28:18-20, could also rightly be translated "As you are going," instead of just "Go.'" So whether you are going on a train, going to the store, or going to work, you should be ready for an opportunity to share a good word about Christ.

Eszti

Jonathan and Corrine Long are present-day OMS missionaries. In 2009, when they were serving in Budapest, Hungary, they hosted a weekly worship evening at their apartment every Friday night for about twelve teens and young adults. One evening, Jonathan asked the members of the group if they believed they were children of God (John 1:12). One young woman responded, "I don't know."

The owner of the voice was a seventeen-year-old girl named Eszter. She was tall and skinny with pale skin and dark hair and eyes. She was shy, yet friendly, and had made friends with some of the group the previous summer by attending an English camp ministry. In the fall, she had started coming to the Longs' apartment for the Friday night meetings and was soon bringing her fifteen-year-old brother, David. They both began to come to the local church service as well.

Jonathan wanted to hear the story behind the response, so he walked Eszter and David to their train stop after the session was over. Eszter, whose nickname is Eszti, began to relate her experience with God. When she was younger, her parents had been part of a historic church in Hungary. Her father was well known for his guitar-playing ability. A rich member of the church bought him a guitar so he could play on Sunday mornings.

Her family had fallen on hard times, however, so her father had taken a second job playing at a Hungarian folk restaurant in the tourist district of Budapest. When members of the church found out he was using the guitar outside of the church, they took it back and asked the family to leave the church. The family was devastated by the loss of the father's job and the loss of their church home.

Shortly after this event, Eszti was surfing YouTube when she came across a ministry video depicting the crucifixion of Christ. Following the video was an explanation of sin and instructions on how one could repent and be saved. Because she was a receptive person of peace, Eszti felt convicted by the video, so she prayed the prayer in the video and went in search of the family Bible. She was the only person in her family to read the Bible.

After hearing her story, Jonathan continued to question Eszti about why she was still unsure about being a child of God. She thought for a moment and then replied, "I try to do the right things, but sometimes I do things that I don't think God would like. How do I know he still loves me?"

In response to her question, Jonathan talked to Eszti about God's grace, until it was time for David and her to catch the train. He prayed that the seeds he had planted about grace and forgiveness would take root in Eszti and that she would recognize herself as a child of God.

The following Sunday, David and Eszti came to the church service and asked to speak to Jonathan. David told him that he had become a child of God. Eszti explained that David had heard their conversation on the way to the train station. He had been asking himself the same questions about faith that Eszti had been asking, but they had never talked about it. He thought about the conversation all day on Saturday until he finally prayed to the Lord for salvation, kneeling down on the floor of his bedroom, all alone. Eszti had also pondered the encouraging words that Jonathan had shared with her on the way to the train. She too had come to the happy conclusion that she was a child of God and had renewed her allegiance to him since the Friday meeting.

After that special weekend, both Eszti and David rarely missed church or the Friday meetings. They both grew in their faith and became active in sharing their testimonies with others. Several weeks later, Eszti and David showed up at church with two other people. The joy on their faces was evident for everyone to see. They had brought their mom and dad.

Both Eszti and David were receptive persons of peace. Eszti just needed more reassurance and understanding of the Bible to become confidant in her faith. David too was ready to make a commitment to Christ, but he needed more biblical understanding, and he needed to have his questions answered. They both needed Jonathan Long, God's faithful witness, to be there for them. God used Jonathan to reach out to them, sow the seeds of the Gospel, and show them the way back to God.

Jonathan listened to the prompting of the Holy Spirit to walk Eszti and David to the train station that evening so that he could give Eszti more guidance on her way to understanding faith and forgiveness. Eszti then became a bridge to her brother, David, and also to her parents. A new stream of salvation was birthed. Jonathan did not have any idea that David needed to hear his message as much as Eszti did. Only God knew that it was a divine appointment for David that night. God used Jonathan's conversation with Eszti to bring David into the kingdom of God.

This same scenario may happen to you, or perhaps it already has. Sometimes, you may think you are witnessing to one person, when it is the quiet friend who is listening nearby whose life you may be touching just as much or even more.

The Interpreter

Deanna Cathcart is also a present-day missionary with OMS and has traveled extensively to different countries, holding seminars and conferences for young people, with a focus on sexual purity. Deanna is passionate about soul winning. She believes that when you are on a mission trip – whether you are going to paint a building or lead a youth conference – your main purpose is still to search for persons of peace.

In 2005, Deanna led a team of women on a mission trip to Brazil. The trip included a speaking engagement at a conference for about four hundred women. Deanna needed a knowledgeable interpreter for those meetings. The mission team hired a fluent man who was the director of an English school nearby.

Because of the tight schedule, the team had no time to meet with the interpreter before the conference began. The first night, the church was packed, and the man was nervous because he was not used to speaking before large crowds. To make matters worse, the first speaker of the evening had never used an interpreter before. When speaking with an interpreter, you have to remember to speak in phrases or with pauses and to give the interpreter plenty of time to translate. The speaker forgot all these points, so the frustrated interpreter couldn't keep up with her or remember all the points she was making.

Then there was another problem. The speaker used a lot of Scripture passages, but the interpreter had difficulty finding them in the Bible he was given to use. Another man had to be on the stage to help him find the passages. This situation made the speech long and embarrassing for everyone. When the evening was finally over, the interpreter was exhausted both mentally and emotionally.

Deanna made her way over to the embarrassed man and asked him if she could meet with him to prepare for the next night. They set aside two hours to go over her material. He was grateful and readily agreed, but when he learned that her topic would be sexual purity, he again became stressed and uncomfortable. He would be on stage before all those young people talking about sex and STDs? He nearly backed out of his commitment to translate, but Deanna reassured him and took him through the lesson.

Deanna has a dynamic way of speaking. She asked the interpreter to repeat not only her words but also to mimic her movements and her passion as she was speaking. He laughed, but he agreed to try. The more they talked, the more he felt ready to translate.

The service later that night impacted not only the audience, but Deanna's translator as well. He and Deanna worked smoothly like a team that had been together for a long time. But Deanna's heart had become concerned about the man's salvation, especially when she witnessed his difficulty in finding biblical passages the night before. Deanna knew she could not leave the country without talking to this man about his soul, so she took him aside after the service.

Deanna thanked the interpreter for his service and told him how much God loved him and how nothing could keep him from God's love. She also asked him to let her know when he became a Christian. Quickly he put his hand out as if to stop her and said, "Please. You are going to make me start crying." Suddenly, Deanna knew this was a divine appointment, so she asked the man if he would like to receive Christ right at that moment. With tears in his eyes, he told her, "Yes."

They prayed together, and that night his name was written in the Book of Life. Deanna's belief that the main purpose of life is to find persons of peace is so true. She thought she would find these persons of peace in the young people attending the conference. Instead, she found her person of peace in a middle-aged interpreter who "just happened" to be the director of an entire school. The man was ready to pray; he just needed to be asked. His willingness to be receptive to the Word of God opened up hundreds of connections to other people in his school. His changed life had the potential to impact hundreds of families for Christ.

God knew where to put a faithful witness like Deanna Cathcart so that she could cross paths with a receptive man who could be a bridge to so many more. But this story is important not only for the mission field but also for the everyday business of our daily lives. Always be ready to share your faith in Christ. You never know when you will encounter a person of peace who is ready to pray and just needs to be asked if they want to receive Christ.

The Muslim Villagers

Yusuf is a present-day evangelist and church planter who ministers in partnership with OMS. The nation he is working in cannot be identified because he could be arrested for spreading the Gospel there. Yusuf bravely goes about searching for persons of peace through the guidance and direction of the Holy Spirit.

He lays his life on the line day after day in hopes of making an eternal difference in the lives of others.

One day, Yusuf and a coworker met some ladies in a village marketplace, where the Holy Spirit prompted him to speak to the women about Jesus. A zealous Muslim man overheard their conversation and immediately set about disrupting and opposing them. Yusuf and his coworker did not cower in the face of this hostile attack, nor did they fear for their safety or freedom. Instead, they boldly acknowledged the power and authority of the Lord Jesus Christ. They held out their Bibles and told the Muslim man that they possessed the living and authoritative Word of God. They proclaimed to all the people in the marketplace that the Bible is the true Word of God and that the proof of all that they were saying is written inside its pages.

The Muslim man scoffed loudly at Yusuf's words and claimed that the Bible was full of lies and treachery. By this time, a crowd was gathering to hear the exchange. The man said that the Bible proclaimed a false god and that it set loose demons. He raised his voice in triumph and yelled, "The Qur'an is God's word, and Allah and his prophet Mohammed are the only true bearers of truth!"

Yusuf and his coworker could not let the Muslim man's words stand. They immediately began to call on God to defend the honor of his name. Emboldened by the Holy Spirit, they told the Muslim man to bring out his Qur'an and let God decide which holy book is the true account of the living God. He quickly ran to get it and returned. Now the crowd in the marketplace was really excited.

The men of God laid their Bible on the ground and issued a challenge: "If you believe that the Bible is not the Word of the living God, trample on it with your foot. But be warned. The living Word is a consuming fire and will consume those who trample upon and dishonor it. Now, lay your Qur'an on the ground and similarly allow us to trample upon it. Together, we will agree to call upon the living God to decide which one is the true, living Word of God."

In the presence of the crowd, the Muslim man brazenly and defiantly agreed to the challenge. The men of God held hands in a circle around the Bible and the Qur'an and asked God to reveal himself. Undeterred, the Muslim man slandered the Word of God and literally trampled upon the Bible. He said over and over that it was filled with rubbish. The men of God then each in turn went to the Qur'an and gently placed their foot on it and declared it to be filled with deceit.

After this challenge, they picked up their respective books and went home. Yusuf left that village the next morning, but three days later he received a phone call. A Christian coworker from that village called to tell him that the very night of the challenge, the Muslim man fell sick and progressively deteriorated. Christians went to him and begged him to repent and call upon Jesus, but he defiantly and stubbornly refused. On the third day, he died. The news spread rapidly throughout the entire village. The living God had defended the integrity of his Word. The villagers were astounded, and as a result, many were coming to the Christians and asking them how to be saved. Revival had come.

The story of Yusuf – a modern-day power encounter – is similar to the encounter on Mount Carmel in the Old Testament, found in 1 Kings 18. In that chapter, the prophet Elijah held a contest between himself and the prophets of the false god Baal. They each sacrificed a bull on an altar and prayed for it to be burned up. In a mighty display of power, the one true God of Elijah sent fire from heaven and completely consumed the bull as well as the twelve barrels of water that he had poured into a trench around the altar. In this Old Testament account, the one to whom the miracle was given readily believed, and many more were converted who saw the miracle.

Yusuf was diligently searching for a person of peace, and he was faithfully sowing seeds of the Gospel. Unfortunately, in this present-day story, the Muslim man refused to believe and a contest resulted. Once again, God gave the people a miraculous display of his power. The manifestation of God's power came like a flood, and many in the village showed themselves to be persons of peace as a result and became believers.

Just as in the days of old, God is the same yesterday, today, and forever. God knew there were people in that village who longed to know him and were earnestly searching for the truth. He is a God of signs and wonders, and he will do what is needed to prove himself and reconcile with persons of peace.

Yusuf and his coworkers are true heroes of the faith. They risk their lives every day so that others may live with Jesus in eternity. We need to ask God to fill us all with that kind of courage and unselfishness. We often worry about offending someone or being rejected, while many like Yusuf witness under circumstances that could bring about their death or imprisonment at any moment. God help us to have the character of Yusuf.

Chapter 4

A Person of Peace Is Well-Known

Persons of peace are well-known individuals who have a reputation in their community. They may be known for something spectacular that they have accomplished, or they may be famous for their wealth and power. Often they are leaders in business or government. Perhaps they have made a name for themselves in education or the arts. The type of reputation they have can vary greatly, but the bottom line is this: they are able to influence a lot of other people in some way. People of reputation may be good or bad; either way, we know who they are, and we will listen to them.

God uses men and women of reputation to sow seeds for his kingdom and to reap a harvest of believers, because they can draw crowds who will listen to their message. They often help to fund the expansion of ministries in a given area. They may also use their connections to influence others for Christ in business and government. God uses these people to grant visas for God's messengers, to donate property for ministerial purposes, to get permission from city elders for evangelistic outreaches, and so much more. They are often used to birth ideas that aid in the spreading of the Word through their wealth, power, fame, education, or character.

The following stories describe persons of peace who are

people of reputation. The illustrations are from biblical personalities, pioneer missionaries of earlier days, and some of today's witnesses. Their stories show the powerful help that people of reputation can give in the spreading of the Gospel.

Biblical Characters

Sergius Paulus

During the time of Jesus, most of the known world was divided into provinces under Roman rule. Every province had a governor who had many responsibilities. He was in charge of levying and collecting taxes, minting more money when needed, and sending reports to the emperor or his representative. He was in charge of the local authorities and could administer justice if needed in special cases. He commanded Roman military forces, which included many legions of men in his province. A governor had numerous assistants, staff members, and an advisory council. He knew and was known by everyone of importance in his province.

Sergius Paulus was the governor of the island of Cyprus during the time of Paul's first missionary journey (Acts 13:4-12). Paul, Barnabas, and John Mark had been sent out by the church at Antioch under the direction of the Holy Spirit to minister to the people of Cyprus, which was Barnabas's homeland. The men traveled all over the island, preaching about Jesus, until they came to Paphos, where the governor resided.

Sergius Paulus employed a sorcerer named Bar-Jesus, also known as Elymas. It was not uncommon for Roman leaders to have sorcerers in their employ, especially those who had the specific gifts of prophecy or healing. These gifts were highly prized then as they still are today, as people go to fortune-tellers and mediums.

Sergius Paulus sent for Paul because he wanted to learn

about Jesus, but Elymas tried to prevent the governor from fully understanding what Paul had to say. Through the power of the Holy Spirit, Paul recognized at once that they were dealing with a false prophet and a man of evil. God gave Paul the gift of discernment for that place and time. He did not back down at all. In fact, the Scriptures say that Paul looked Elymas in the eye and spoke directly to the sorcerer and said, *"O full of all deceit and fraud, you son of the devil, you enemy of all righteousness, will you not cease perverting the straight ways of the Lord? And now, indeed, the hand of the Lord is upon you, and you shall be blind, not seeing the sun for a time"* (Acts 13:10-11). Immediately, a mist came over the man's eyes and he was blinded. He began to grope about and beg someone to lead him. The Lord indeed had taken his eyesight in an instant.

That was all it took for the governor. He was convinced that the missionaries were speaking the truth when he saw this amazing display of God's power right before his eyes. The Scriptures say that he believed that day and became a follower of Jesus. The Bible also says that their teachings astonished him (Acts 13:12).

As you can see, Sergius Paulus was an incredible man of reputation and influence in Rome. God knew his heart and knew he was a seeker. God also knew what far-reaching effects his redemption could have on the nation on so many levels. As a provincial governor, he could open doors of opportunity that would take missionaries years of hard work to open. He would be in the company of other men of reputation in business, government, and the military, where he could share his knowledge of Jesus and then have them pass on the same knowledge to others. God could use him as an incredible bridge to others because he was such a man of reputation.

This story is unique from the perspective of the witnesses too. Most of the time in searching for persons of peace, we are polite, loving, gracious, and kind. But Paul demonstrated that when we are confronted with evil and when that evil is trying to halt our message, it is appropriate to take on that evil and perform spiritual warfare on the spot.

We can and must battle the Enemy for souls. It is important, therefore, to be prepared spiritually when we go out in search of persons of peace. The people of Antioch fasted and prayed mightily before sending Paul and his companions on their journey, and they functioned as prayer warriors for the missionaries throughout their journey. Do not take prayer for granted, because it is a powerful tool for us to use to get the job done for the Lord.

How is your prayer life? Have you recruited people to pray for you and your ministry? Prayer paves the way for effective ministry to happen. As evangelists, prayers of protection are important because attacks by the Enemy will come when we begin to encroach upon the Devil's territory in battle for a lost soul. Ask God for the discernment of Paul, the encouragement of Barnabas, and the influential heart of Sergius Paulus.

Lydia

Paul did not let gender or cultural boundaries stop him in his search for persons of peace. If he had, Lydia might never have heard the good news of Jesus, and the wonderful church at Philippi might never have been started. The biblical record of the salvation of Lydia is found in Acts 16:11-15. On Paul's second missionary journey, Silas, Timothy, and Luke accompanied him as he traveled to Philippi, a Roman colony in Macedonia. Philippi was a major city and a main transportation gateway connecting the eastern provinces with Italy.

Again and again, the Lord sent the early missionaries to places where many cultures and races intermingled. They often went to port cities like Philippi where new converts would travel with the news of the Gospel to faraway lands. God, with his foreknowledge, knew where he had persons of peace who were seeking him and who would spread the news far and wide.

When Paul and his followers came to Philippi, they searched out a prayer group that met by the river on the Sabbath. The meeting was held just outside the city gates and was attended by a small group of women, among whom was a business owner named Lydia. Because Lydia dealt with purple cloth (a costly material), she most likely was a wealthy merchant. Her customers would have been the nobility of the land who could pay a higher price for cloth than the common laborer could pay. Her standing in the community as a wealthy businesswoman would have made Lydia a person of influence and reputation in her community, especially among the women.

The Bible says that Lydia worshiped God already. She was a Gentile, but she had been meeting with other ladies to pray to the God of the Jews. She truly was a seeker and believed in God; however, she did not know Jesus. As Paul spoke, the Lord opened Lydia's heart, and she believed. As the women listened to the sounds of the water in the river nearby, the living water of the truth of God flowed into their ears as well. The Holy Spirit draws people to the Lord and convicts and enlightens their hearts.

Lydia desired to be baptized right away. The Bible does not mention a husband, and Lydia appears to have been the head of her household. The fact that she could house four other men and provide for these many guests with apparent ease is another indication that she was wealthy. Because the missionaries were traveling by faith with no money or means of support, they always appreciated the hospitality of those who offered it. With Lydia's encouragement and enthusiasm and, most importantly, the Holy Spirit speaking through Paul, we read in verse 15 that other members of her household were saved and baptized too. A new house church was born.

Lydia is just the kind of person of peace described by Jesus in our foundational passages (Matthew 10:1-42, Mark 6:7-13, and Luke 10:1-24). She received the message and the messengers with gladness. Her first act as a new believer was to open her home and practice the gift of hospitality. She was also evangelistically minded and desired that her whole family follow Jesus. As head of her household, she encouraged the others to hear and to believe. She showed a beautiful servant's heart from the beginning, and she did not allow her wealth to give her a reason to be haughty. She was willing to share what she had with the missionaries, so she opened her home and her pantry of food.

Lydia would have great opportunities to share the Gospel with more than just her family. Through her business of selling purple cloth, she would have opportunities to converse with many people in Philippi, especially the wealthy class. She interacted regularly with women in the market at her place of business, and that would open many opportunities for sharing her testimony and sharing about Christ.

Paul, as God's witness, also set a wonderful example for us in approaching this group of ladies by the riverside. In his former life, Paul was a respected Jewish teacher and high-standing Pharisee who would never have approached a group of women, especially on the bank of a river. But Paul had learned that every person – man, woman, or child – deserved to be a child of God through the blood of Christ, and he was determined to share the Gospel message with everyone he encountered. Sometimes he spoke in synagogues, but most often he spoke anywhere God gave him an opportunity. He no longer spoke just to pious Jewish men; he now shared with anyone who would listen, including women.

We too must be ready and willing to share with anyone,

anywhere – inside or outside; rich or poor; male or female; young or old. God may have many persons of peace ready to hear your message from every walk of life.

Zacchaeus

Just as a woman like Lydia could be a person of reputation in biblical times, so could a despised tax collector like Zacchaeus (Luke 19:1-10). Zacchaeus lived in Jericho and was the chief tax collector for the region. Under Roman rule, the Jews paid a heavy allotment of taxes. The Jews greatly resented these taxes because they were used to support a secular government that included the worship of pagan gods.

Tax collectors were among the most despised people in the country. Even though they were Jews by birth, they were considered the lowest of traitors because they had chosen to work for the oppressors. Tax collectors were also notorious for gouging their own people and getting rich from the added profits.

Zacchaeus was apparently one of these wealthy cheaters and was known for his bad reputation. However, even though he was a traitor, a cheat, and a liar, Jesus loved him. Jesus did not follow social norms in avoiding the company of a tax collector. Instead, he went straight up to Zacchaeus and broke tradition by entering into his home. Jesus demonstrated in a public way that we are to reach out to the "untouchables" in our societies. Jesus saw the potential in him to be a powerful person of peace, a man of reputation who could influence others.

Zacchaeus felt the love of the Lord and responded to it in a beautiful and miraculous way. In a spontaneous show of true repentance, he began to promise joyful restitution to all those from whom he had stolen. Zacchaeus promised outright to give half of his wealth to the poor and to restore fourfold what he had stolen from others by charging higher taxes. Jesus then proclaimed him to be a true son of Abraham and said that salvation had come to his house.

Known as the despicable tax collector, he was probably the least likely person that anyone thought would become a righteous man. Zacchaeus was a man who was known far and wide in his position. Everyone knew who the tax collectors were, and he had dealings with nearly everyone in carrying out his seedy business. Now he could use those relationships to initiate new conversations about the cleansing and life-changing power of Jesus. The news of the change in Zacchaeus was sure to spread far and wide and gave him a huge platform for reaching a big audience. We cannot see inside a soul, but God knows the hearts of men. Our responsibility is to give the good news to all, regardless of what terrible things we know about them.

Zacchaeus was known to be a sinner in his community and was despised and reviled. Were the people who were serving God in that area praying for his salvation? Had anyone been speaking truth and light into his life? Did any person shed tears over his lost condition and agonize in prayer for his lost soul? It is important to keep the lost in our prayers. Make a list of lost people that you know and begin to pray for them daily. Pray for divine appointments for seed-sowing into their lives. Can you look beyond the sin and reach out to the sinner? Can you love the unlovely?

Saul of Tarsus

One ordinary day became extraordinary in the life of a witness named Ananias. As he was going about his daily routine in Damascus, a vision from God suddenly filled his eyes, and God called him by name (Acts 9:1-22). Ananias recognized the voice of the Lord immediately and responded, "Yes, Lord." From that moment on, his life and the life of Saul of Tarsus would never be the same. God chose these two men to play an important role in spreading the Gospel of Jesus to the nations.

Ananias's role, as explained to him in his vision, was to seek out Saul of Tarsus, who was staying with a man named Judas on Straight Street. God wanted Ananias to place his hands on Saul and restore his sight. Ananias's first response to this command was to show God his fear about carrying out this task. He had heard about Saul's persecution of the Christians, and he was afraid for his own life. He knew that Saul had the authority from the chief priests to arrest anyone who followed Jesus.

God's response was to proclaim Saul as his chosen servant who would carry the name of the Lord before the Gentiles, their kings, and the people of Israel. In essence, God told Ananias not to worry about his own safety but to carry out his command to go to Saul. Then the Lord added with a compassionate voice: *"For I will show him how many things he must suffer for My name's sake"* (Acts 9:16).

Ananias did not argue or delay any further. He made his way to Straight Street, determined to obey the Lord no matter the cost. Faith and belief in God won the battle of his heart because when Ananias got to Saul, he called him "Brother" (Acts 9:17). Ananias then delivered the message from the Lord, and immediately something like scales fell from Saul's eyes. He was baptized right then and began his new life in Christ.

Saul's role was to respond to the visions that God used to capture his attention and to become the person of peace that God intended him to be. Saul already had a miraculous encounter on the Damascus Road a few days earlier. The Lord was preparing his heart for salvation because he was a true seeker of the truth, even if he had been caught up in the persecution of Christians.

Here again was an unlikely convert in the eyes of believers. Saul was trained by the famous Gamaliel, a prestigious teacher in Judaism. He was a Pharisee of the highest order. Although he was a Jew, Saul was also a Roman citizen, enjoying all the rights and privileges of the ruling class.

God's words in Acts 9:16 were fulfilled and Saul, renamed Paul a little later, went on to travel extensively throughout the Roman Empire, preaching the Gospel. As hard as he had tried to stamp out the Christian movement, he worked three times harder trying to build it up. As a person of peace who was a man of reputation, Paul did, in fact, go on to preach to high-ranking Roman officials as well as high-ranking Jewish leaders. He went on three successful missionary journeys to Gentile lands and wrote the majority of the letters that now make up our New Testament.

Paul also planted churches, mentored Christian leaders, and encouraged the faithful with visits and letters. He helped settle disputes of doctrine at the first church conferences. He performed many miracles, signs, and wonders. And yes, he also suffered. He was beaten, imprisoned, and forced to flee for his life from towns where he had once been respected and honored. He suffered from the cold and from lack of food. However, he demonstrated remarkable endurance and even sang songs of praise to God while shackled in a prison dungeon. He is known by such names as the Apostle of Faith and the Apostle to the Gentiles.

Ananias obeyed the voice of the Lord and went in search of a person of peace that morning in Damascus. He didn't let fear of his safety, fear of the loss of his freedom, or even fear of death stop him from witnessing for our King. We should all try to be like Ananias. Think about your relationship with God. Are you living close to him so that you can hear his voice? Are you spending time with the Lord so that he has opportunities to speak to you? Would you be willing to go even if you felt he was sending you into a risky situation?

Historical Pioneer Missionaries

Jager Afrikaner

History records with great detail the pioneer missionary adventures of Robert Moffat, who arrived at Cape Town, South Africa, in 1817. Moffat and his wife, Mary, had a perilous career in several areas of South Africa for many decades. They not only battled resistant tribes, but they also constantly battled the government of South Africa, which saw the Moffats' liberating Gospel of equality among men as a threat to their way of life.

In their early years, the Moffats managed to live only for a few months in the same location before the governor over the area would demand that they leave. These forced moves were discouraging, frustrating, and dangerous because they were often accompanied by robberies. While the Moffats were preaching in one place, their home would be ransacked at the same time by the very ones they were trying so desperately to lead to Jesus.

After one move, however, the Lord graciously sent the Moffats to an area where John Ebner, another brave young missionary, was working. The Moffats and Ebner became friends and ministry partners. For five years, Ebner had been ministering in an area that was near the tribal lands of Jager Afrikaner, a notorious outlaw chief. The Moffats were given permission to settle among Afrikaner's people.

Many years earlier, Afrikaner had been a slave and was treated with great cruelty by his South African owners. He managed to escape and settled with his family near the Orange River. Soon hundreds of his people joined him, and he led them in predatory warfare for many years. They attacked colony farmers as well as neighboring tribes. The plundering and killing was so devastating that the South African government put a huge bounty on his head. Afrikaner was one of the most feared and wanted men in South Africa.

In his infinite wisdom, God had been preparing Robert Moffat for this meeting with Afrikaner for several years. His reputation as a reformer and a believer in equality preceded him wherever he went. Afrikaner's reputation for stimulating loyalty among his followers preceded him also. And God understood Afrikaner's heart and what drove him to commit his violent acts. God set the stage for the birth of a powerful person of peace.

Under the Moffats' influence and persistence, Jager Afrikaner made a life-transforming commitment to Jesus. Because he was a chief, his influence over his followers was the break the missionaries so badly needed for their work to be victorious. The news of Afrikaner's conversion traveled to Cape Town, but few believed it could be true. In the ensuing months, however, through Afrikaner's power and influence among his people, many of his tribe were also converted. He is the perfect example of how God can use a person of reputation, even a *bad* reputation, to further his kingdom.

The next year, Robert Moffat traveled to Cape Town and took Afrikaner with him. Afrikaner went with great personal risk because he was still a wanted man. Moffat introduced Afrikaner to the governor, and his lordship was so impressed that he presented Afrikaner with a wagon worth eighty pounds sterling, a sum equal to a year's salary for a skilled laborer. He was also given a pardon, 100 pounds, and the promise of safe passage back home.

The following year, the Lord directed the Moffats to move to another place of ministry that was quite far away. One day, to their amazement, Afrikaner pulled up to their home in his magnificent wagon. It was loaded with all the possessions they had to leave behind and many other gifts. God blessed both of these men with an enduring friendship.

Afrikaner was a person of peace and a man of reputation – a bad reputation. He was a famous murderer and robber. He was known for vicious evil in revenge for his past, and he caused countless others to suffer at his hands. Nevertheless, God was able to redeem him and change him completely. After being cleansed from his sins, Afrikaner used his great influence and power for good.

This illustration should inspire us to search for persons of peace even among the vilest of humanity. The power of God to transform a sinner steeped in the darkness of sin is amazing. The Enemy's bondage over a life may seem like impenetrable chains, but it is no match for the blood of Christ that can wash away all sin and make new creations from the most improbable of souls.

Namakei

John Paton, a Scotsman, became the most famous missionary to ever serve in the South Pacific. At the age of twelve, he dedicated himself to the Lord's service, and from that day forward he was a force for God. As an adult, he volunteered to be a missionary to the New Hebrides islands. Amid much opposition, one man told him that he would be eaten by cannibals. Paton's response was: "If I can just live and die serving and honoring the Lord Jesus, it doesn't make much difference whether I am eaten by cannibals or eaten by worms. In the day of resurrection, my body will still rise as fair as yours in the image of our great Redeemer, Jesus Christ."

In 1858, Paton and his wife, Mary Ann, journeyed to the islands. The violence and debauchery of the people were shocking. One day they heard musket fire and war cries nearby as a fight to the death broke out between feuding tribes. Later that night there was dancing and feasting as the victorious tribe ate the bodies of the dead. This was their initiation to life on the islands. A few months later, John grieved as his wife and infant son died shortly after childbirth.

Several times, Paton was confronted and threatened by those involved in witchcraft and sorcery. On one occasion, the people tried to poison him, but John boldly ate the poisoned fruit and told the crowd that he would prove that his God was stronger than their gods. He promised the people that he would not die, and that if he returned, they must admit that his God, Jehovah, was the true and living God. Sure enough, he did not die, and several days later he walked back to the village in perfect health. Many of the people were willing to sit and listen to him teach that day. However, Paton still needed a powerful breakthrough, a person of peace who would help break the satanic strongholds of the islands.

Paton returned home for a year of fundraising. While he was home, he married a devout Christian lady named Margaret. They soon returned to an island named Aniwa in the New Hebrides chain. It was on this island that Paton met the Lord's designated person of peace. He was the chief of the island, a man named Namakei.

John began reaching out in friendship to Namakei, all the while praying that he might be a person of peace. Some of Namakei's people were friendlier to the missionaries, but the chief's brother was the highest-ranking sorcerer, and he tried to shoot Paton on two different occasions. Some of Namakei's people guarded the Patons' home so it was not set on fire at night.

As Paton steadily walked and preached in village after village, some of the people began to turn to the Lord. The people practiced fewer revenge killings and child sacrifices. However, the real breakthrough came when Paton began to dig a well.

The island did not have a good fresh-water supply. Paton told

Namakei that he was going to dig deep in the earth to see if God would give them fresh water from the ground. The island did not have any wells, so the chief thought that Paton must have lost his mind. Namakei begged Paton to stop such foolishness for his reputation's sake. But Paton kept digging and praying. After he had dug to around thirty feet, the earth began to feel damp. Paton excitedly told the people that he would find fresh water the next day. Namakei again begged him to stop and was fearful that he would fall into the ocean and be eaten by sharks.

The next day, Paton did indeed reach fresh water. Many people gathered around in amazement, and the chief took the first drink. He declared that it was fresh, like rain. Paton told them that Jehovah had sent the people this water. "No God has ever done anything like this for us," said Namakei. "Will you share this water with us, or is it only for your family?"

"Jehovah gives it to all of you." Paton declared. "He gives many good gifts, but best of all is the gift of his Son, as I have told you."

Then Paton watched a miracle unfold. Namakei spoke to his people at the well on the following Sunday. He spoke with power and flourished a tomahawk for emphasis. He told all the people that Jehovah had proven himself to be God. He stomped his feet and beat his chest, crying out that he believed that Jehovah was the true God and that he would now worship only him.

Then Namakei challenged all the people to bring their idols and throw them in a pile to be burned. He exhorted all the people to learn the right way to live from Paton so that they could all go to live with the true God, Jehovah, after they died. The people went running for their idols and burned them in a huge fire, all the while chanting "Jehovah! Jehovah! Jehovah!"

After all the years of challenging sacrifice and dangerous persecution, Paton was in awe of how God had answered his prayers. Over the next few years, every single person on the island became a follower of Jesus Christ.

Namakei is an excellent example of a person of peace having a reputation. He was a respected chief on the island of Aniwa. He was considered to be wise, and people followed his example. So when he believed, he was able to be a powerful influence on the rest of his tribe.

John Paton exemplifies the courage and spirit of the early pioneer missionaries. Despite danger and threats, many sorrows, and few converts for many years, he persevered in his search for persons of peace among the people living on the New Hebrides islands. He continued loving and reaching out to people who lived in terrible darkness, and finally the light of Jesus pierced that darkness and banished it.

Many people are living in terrible darkness near you. Please pray to the Lord of the harvest for workers who are willing to reach out to them. May each of us have the courage and perseverance of John Paton to find these persons of peace no matter what the cost.

Yang, Champion Boxer

Jonathan Goforth and his wife, Rosalind, became missionaries to China in the late 1880s. They suffered hardship, persecution, and danger, and Jonathan was nearly killed during the Boxer Rebellion. But the suffering did not deter their ministry. Goforth's unceasing energy in preaching the Gospel is incomparable. History records that he would often preach for eight hours a day to crowds of up to twenty-five thousand people.

The meetings were often charged with emotion. The Holy Spirit would come in a mighty way, and people would weep in repentance and conviction, fall to their knees, and often give public confession of their sins. Goforth traveled all over China holding revival meetings, and multitudes came to Jesus for the first time. Thousands of Christians came into a deeper relationship with Christ in spiritual renewal as well.

The Goforths focused their missionary work in the Henan Province, and for many years they lived in the city of Anyang. Still today, the seeds of their work and the fruit of their labors for Jesus continue. Fewer than 100 Christians lived in Anyang before the days of revival a century ago. Now, one in ten people in that city of two million are believers.

God sent a special person of peace to Jonathan Goforth in his ministry. He was a man of reputation because he was a famous boxer named Yang. At the height of his career, he was the greatest prizefighter in the entire region. Even more amazing, he had never once been knocked out. Although he had many loyal fans, some people held a grudge against him because they lost money in betting against him.

When the news spread that Yang had become a Christian at one of Goforth's revival meetings, his enemies saw an opportunity to get revenge. One day in the marketplace, men surrounded him and beat him so badly that he almost did not survive the attack. The missionaries encouraged him to go to the police, but Yang refused to press charges. A few months later, his enemies again tried to kill him as he walked around the town. He was beaten so severely that for months his family did not know whether he would survive. His recovery was slow, but still he did not want to press charges.

After Yang was completely healed from these attacks, he began to go all around the area preaching the Gospel. He was so well known that many would listen to him with excitement and great curiosity. God used this man of reputation to bring many to salvation. He traveled in spite of the danger to himself. He had twice recovered from beatings that would have killed an ordinary man. However, Yang was unafraid to go out and face more attacks for the sake of the Gospel. He used his famous name to get people in many places to listen to him.

Even though he was a prizewinning boxer, Yang refused to return violence with violence. Through this lesson, the Lord used him in such a great way that he even led many of his former enemies to Christ. He died a few years later, but he left behind a church of six hundred members in his town and ten other churches in surrounding villages.

A person of peace can be a tremendous blessing to the work of the Lord. A person's fame, their reputation, opens doors for the sharing of his or her testimony. People love to have heroes and to seek out celebrities whenever one is near. Sometimes people will throng together and be willing to wait for hours to get a glimpse of a "star."

We should never hesitate to present the Gospel to a well-known person whom the Lord puts in our path. As "ordinary" humans, we may feel intimidated or perhaps even unworthy to give the Gospel to a celebrity. Remember that a famous person is still only a sinner who needs the saving grace of Jesus just like anyone else. Famous people may seem to have everything a person could want, but in reality, they may be lonely, empty, and depressed. Famous people fill our alcoholic and drug rehabilitation facilities just as quickly as ordinary citizens. They feel the same emotions and struggle with the same questions of life that all people do. Most importantly, they too will suffer the same judgment if they refuse God's Son. So do not be afraid to go for it if God puts a celebrity in your path.

Chai Cho-si

Reverend Samuel A. Moffett went to Korea as a young man, full of zeal in proclaiming the Lord Jesus Christ. He settled in Pyongyang, Korea, in 1893. Pyongyang was the ancient capital city of Korea and is now the capital of North Korea. It is located on the west bank of the Taedong River, about two hundred miles north of Seoul, the capital of South Korea.

Moffett soon became well known for his sweet character, and he always attracted a lot of attention because of his height, his blond hair, and his blue eyes, which were all in stark contrast to the Koreans. Crazy tales spread quickly throughout the area because people viewed Moffett as an oddity, something like a novelty they would come to see at a carnival. Crowds came to his house daily in hopes of getting a glimpse of "The Foreigner." So many people came that they blocked the road in front of his house every day with their oxcarts.

Moffett didn't mind the attention and saw his notoriety as a gift from God. His home became the "stage" while his "performance" was preaching the Gospel. However, he was not an actor playing a dramatic role; he was genuinely telling the stories of God's Word to these first-time listeners.

God sent Moffett a person of peace during these days of home preaching. Among those who came to see him was an important business owner in the city named Chai Cho-si, a popular saloon keeper who had a charismatic personality. Chai Cho-si's saloon bore a blue flag that was split down the middle. This flag signified that he had liquor to sell. Chai Cho-si knew many people in the community because men from all walks of life flocked to his place every day to drink.

Chai Cho-si came to Moffett's house again and again. At first, he came to see the strange white-haired giant. Then he came to hear the missionary's exciting stories so he could recount them to his customers for entertainment. Gradually a relationship began to form between the two men because Chai Cho-si was receptive and asking questions. Over time, the message of the Gospel became dear to his sinful heart, and he believed. As a man of reputation, well known and well loved, Chai Cho-si became a wonderful asset to Moffett, becoming his right-hand man. He closed the saloon and gave much time to spreading the Gospel to all his friends, neighbors, and former customers.

Because of his influence, Chai Cho-si helped Moffett start a new church, which drew a crowd of worshipers every Sunday. As usual, the Devil could not allow the new church to continue, so he stirred up the heart of the magistrate to shut it down. The magistrate told the worshipers to cease because the new religion would not allow the people to properly worship and sacrifice to their dead ancestors. Ancestor worship was the centuries-old custom in Korea and was particularly important on New Year's Day, which was fast approaching. The Christians resisted, so the magistrate sent men to arrest them, beat them, and threaten them with death. Instead of thronging to hear Moffett speak, mobs would now throw rocks at him if he walked down the street. The new church was in turmoil, and Moffett didn't know what to do next.

However, God knew and had a plan far greater than any of them imagined. Right at this time, Chinese warriors came down from the north while Japanese warriors came up from the south, each side armed with rifles. The Chinese-Japanese war of 1894 began. As the armies clashed in Pyongyang, the little company of new believers, including Chai Cho-si, scattered like sheep to the mountains in every direction. Moffett returned to Seoul until things settled down.

When Moffett returned to Pyongyang after the war ended in 1895, he found the city burned to the ground, but he also discovered that the Holy Spirit had been at work through Chai Cho-si. With his charismatic personality, Chai Cho-si had attracted many new believers in the mountains all over the north. The war had been instrumental in making people welcome the message of God's love and the comfort of the Gospel.

The Holy Spirit had kindled a fire in the new church of Pyongyang. Even though the Christians lost most of their possessions, they rejoiced that the news of Jesus had spread during their time of great trials. Like Christians in the first century, they fled as refugees in a war while God was forming them to be pioneer missionaries. That small spark was not quenched, and a fire of revival continued for hundreds of miles in every direction. From the rice plains near the sea to the mountain valleys, the revival in Korea blazed. South Korea is now one of the strongest Christian nations in our world today. Getting news of believers in North Korea is difficult, but we have to trust that God is in control and will not allow the seed of faith in the ancestors of those early Christians to die, in spite of Communist rule.

Chai Cho-si is a great example of a person of peace. He was a man of influence in his city. He possessed a good reputation with both rich and poor. His warm and entertaining personality attracted people to him as a saloon keeper, but God knew he could also use him to attract people to hear the message of His Son, Jesus.

We can learn a lot from Moffett's slow-growing relationship with the saloon keeper. Moffett never turned Chai Cho-si away from his doorstep, even though he knew that the man was coming simply out of curiosity or to get material to use as jokes in his saloon. Moffett still loved Chai Cho-si, welcomed him to his home, and continued to build a relationship as long as Chai Cho-si wanted to return to listen some more.

Sometimes a person of peace is formed slowly, as in this example. In his limited vision, Moffett probably never imagined in the beginning that Chai Cho-si would become so important in spreading the Gospel message in Korea. Only God knew and understood his potential. Our job as witnesses is to keep on loving people and proclaiming the message of Christ as long as someone is willing to listen.

Li Goat-lau

Jim and Lillian Dickson, pioneer missionaries to Formosa, which is now known as Taiwan, often traveled in the mountains to minister to the aboriginal tribes that lived there in the 1920s. Sometimes they rode in a little pushcart, traveling across narrow bridges with no protective barriers and looking down at the perilous depths below. At other times they walked, or more accurately, hiked, for hours to get to another tribe who desperately needed to hear the message of Jesus.

On one such trip to the mountains, the Dicksons' interpreter for that day was a poised and confidant woman named Li Goat-lau. She was the leader of her people, and she sat on the legislature of her province, the highest position a citizen could achieve. She was respected and loved and was a strong power in deciding all the policies of her tribe. She had heard of the Dicksons and their work with other tribes, so she invited them to come and speak to her people. She wanted to know what strange news they were bringing to the island. As a wise leader, she wanted to judge for herself if this information could benefit her people.

Li Goat-lau told the Dicksons the story of her tribe. Her people had lived closely together for centuries in the middle of the island of Formosa. They were too fearful of wild animals to branch out into the unknown parts of the island. However, one brave man left the center of the island to scout out the land and leave a trail for other men to follow. This courageous explorer died soon after his journey from an infection in his foot, but he became the tribe's memorialized hero who greatly enlarged their territory. More than thirty villages sprang up wherever he blazed the trail. The tribe's motto became "Fear not to travel where I have made a way."

That night the Dicksons told the story of Nicodemus, but they couldn't tell if it was having an effect on the people. During the service, a group of men came in, and the Dicksons could see that their appearance disturbed Li Goat-lau. The most commanding and well dressed of the men was a member of the tribe who had been educated in Japan as a doctor. He had become Li Goat-lau's rival for the leadership of the tribe, and the two of them had had many bitter battles. After the service, the Dicksons went to their room and didn't know what would happen the following day.

The next day, Li Goat-lau came to the Dicksons' room and told them that she had visited the doctor early that morning. The Holy Spirit had prompted both of them to follow Christ and to be born again, as was told in the story about Nicodemus the previous night. They had listened and heard the Word of God through the Dicksons. They agreed to forget the past and to start new lives in the Christian way. So the leaders settled the matter together at dawn.

The Dicksons arranged for Li Goat-lau to stay at one of the established churches in another area so that she could learn to read and understand the Bible. She was an ardent student and learned well. When she was ready, she went back to her people, excited to share its truths with her tribe. The people welcomed Li Goat-lau gladly and responded to the Gospel with equal joy. She traveled from village to village, preaching and starting churches. But our Enemy, the Devil, was soon alerted and stirred up a man who ran to the government and told lies about the movement.

Soon, the government took away Li Goat-lau's freedom, restricted her activities by putting her under a form of house arrest, and gave her an ultimatum. If she quit preaching and gave up her Christian ways, she could be as free as she was before. History records that Li Goat-lau replied, "To the end of time, I will not forsake God. I do not speak against the government. I am only teaching my people to be good and keep the laws and stop drinking and doing evil things."

The government finally gave Li Goat-lau permission to hold a small conference in her house. Many people were afraid to come because government officials were watching, but about thirty-five people showed up from various villages of her tribe. The Dicksons came too. The conference was inspiring and Spirit filled. Li Goat-lau spoke passionately for God and implored her people to spread the Gospel to all and not to give in to the pressures of the government. Her parting words to the Dicksons that day were: "A fire has been kindled here that will never go out."

Little by little, Li Goat-lau continued to win the lost around her even though she was homebound. Many of the young men that she led to Jesus went on to Bible schools and became pastors. The revival in her aboriginal tribe also continued through the churches she planted before her house arrest. To this day, Li Goat-lau is known as the spiritual mother of a thousand souls.

Persons of peace often use their influence to teach others to stand strong even in the face of persecution and danger. As is illustrated in this story, any time the Holy Spirit is at work drawing souls to Christ, some form of persecution or challenge will come from the Enemy. During these times of challenge, persons of peace can use their powerful reputations to light the way for the rest, and they can often be a greater influence than the original witness. In this case, the Dicksons brought the message, but Li Goat-lau reaped the harvest and strengthened her people as the tribal leader.

Persons of peace are often out in front of the spiritual battles, leading the charge and setting an example for others to follow. They respond rightly in times of difficulty and inspire and motivate others to continue to follow the Lord no matter what the cost. As you search for persons of peace, you also may experience the blessing of finding a man or woman of influential reputation like Li Goat-lau. This person may become a great source of help and strength to you personally, as well as helping to bring in a great harvest.

The Mandarin of Jiangsu

Gladys Aylward was a woman of great courage who answered God's call and made her way to China against all odds. She had little education, had worked as a housemaid, and had been rejected by the China Inland Mission because she couldn't pass its entrance exam. But Aylward was sure that God had called her to minister in China, so in 1932, she spent her entire life savings for passage to Yancheng in the Jiangsu Province.

For several years, Aylward lived in Yancheng with an older missionary lady, Jeanne Lawson. The women made a living from running an inn, which filled up each night with rough, peasant muleteers. The women shared the story of Jesus with them. When they weren't working at the inn, the women would preach in the marketplaces of the surrounding villages and give medical aid from time to time. Aylward studied hard and became quite fluent in the local language.

Upon Mrs. Lawson's death, Gladys Aylward was left alone, the only European in that part of China. The people thought it unseemly that she should continue to run the inn as a single woman with all the male guests. Also, without Mrs. Lawson's support, the inn did not bring in enough profit to provide Aylward with enough food to live on, let alone provide for the people staying at the inn.

Gladys Aylward was at a point of crisis. Her call was strong to be a missionary pioneer, and she had promised Mrs. Lawson that she would carry on her work. But there seemed no possible way to live in her circumstances. At this critical point, God sent Aylward a person of peace.

Three days after the cook informed her that there was not

enough money for food, Aylward was awakened by a commotion outside the gate. The mandarin of Jiangsu, who was the ruler in charge of keeping law and order in all the villages of the province, stood majestically at her door. He was armed with a long curved sword and accompanied by soldiers who also carried swords. His presence outside her humble inn was astonishing in itself, but his words were even more so as he said, "I have come about your feet."

The ancient custom of binding women's feet had been going on for centuries in China. Men considered small feet on a woman to be a sign of beauty. Beginning in infancy, a baby girl's feet were tightly bound, which caused them to be deformed. Women were crippled and suffered much pain from this practice throughout their lives.

The Chinese government had recently made it illegal to bind women's feet. The mandarin, as a man, could not examine women's feet. As a woman with unbound feet, however, Aylward could inspect their feet without suffering the wrath of jealous husbands. The mandarin offered Gladys food, a mule, and even soldiers to travel with her if she would go from village to village and enforce this new government decree. This offer would solve all her problems. She would have her needs supplied; she would not be sleeping at the inn; and she would have protection and freedom to travel as a pioneer missionary to all the villages in the entire region.

Because of Aylward's innate honesty, she knew that she couldn't accept the mandarin's offer without first seeking his permission to do her missionary work while she journeyed from town to town. Gladys was honest and brave when she replied, "Sir, I will do as you wish, but you must understand that I have come to China to tell your people about the God I worship. As I inspect the women's feet, I will also use the opportunity to preach to the people."

To her great relief and in answer to prayer, the mandarin agreed completely. At the time, he had no religious bias. In the future days of their working relationship, Gladys continued to share the truth of the Gospel with him as God gave her opportunities. The mandarin continued to be an open listener.

Persons of peace come in many different forms. In this instance, the mandarin was a man of awesome reputation. He was known far and wide, yet God put him strategically in the path of this poor unknown witness for Christ who was all alone and facing hunger. The mere necessities of life were slipping from her grasp, and she had no means to survive, let alone minister.

The mandarin did not readily accept the Gospel as many persons of peace do. However, he was receptive to hearing Aylward's message again and again over time. Under the sovereignty of God, the Lord used his reputation to open doors for the preaching of the Gospel in many places. Gladys Aylward was able to touch an entire region of China with the Gospel through the permission of the mandarin. Unfortunately, we do not know whether the mandarin accepted Christ as his Savior in the end. What we do know, however, is that God can use anyone, saved or unsaved, to further his kingdom.

Gladys Aylward led an extraordinary life. Later in her missionary career, she opened orphanages and is best known for leading 100 orphans to safety on a long journey in the midst of war. This deed was immortalized in the 1958 movie *The Inn of the Sixth Happiness,* with Ingrid Bergman playing her role. Through her person of peace, the Chinese government gave Aylward entrance into every village home in her province, supplied her needs, gave her protection to travel as a single woman all alone in a foreign land, and *paid* her to preach the Gospel of Jesus Christ to an entire region of China. All this was provided by a government that did not want her to be there. We serve an amazing God.

You may have a burden for ministry but see no financial way to accomplish your dream. Seek the Lord in prayer and continue to step out in faith in every way that you can. Just like Gladys Aylward, you also may be sent a person of peace, a person of reputation and means, whom God will use to open a door for you to minister.

Present-Day Witnesses

Imam Ali

An imam is an important figure in Muslim communities. He usually leads worship in the mosque, and he leads public prayers. People come to him for spiritual guidance and for teaching from the Qur'an on Fridays. To be an imam, age is not a factor, but one's character and knowledge of Islam and the Qur'an are the most important qualities. Needless to say, an imam is a respected person in the community and a man of high reputation.

This story recently happened in a Muslim community that must remain unidentified because of the danger to the individuals involved. An imam named Ali was a young, strong, passionate follower of Mohammad. But on this day, without symptoms or prior warning, he collapsed unconscious on the floor of the mosque while he was leading the prayers.

Over the next several days, his family took him to doctor after doctor, but no one could discover what was causing his sickness. Days turned into weeks with no improvement. In desperation, his family decided to take him to a variety of witch doctors, but there were still no answers. He only grew progressively worse. Ali felt desperately sick and was unable to sleep. His anxiety continued to rise because he could not get a diagnosis or the correct treatment. His illness did not make any sense, and his family began to suffer because he was unable to work.

One day, he heard a sermon on the radio. The speaker said that Jesus can heal the sick. He told the listeners that if they would turn their lives over to Jesus, the Son of God, they would find his healing touch. That night Ali cried out to Jesus and asked him for healing. In an instant, all of his symptoms were completely gone.

Ali had not been able to sleep well for many weeks, but he asked Jesus to help him sleep. Immediately he fell into a deep and peaceful sleep that lasted for many hours. After Ali woke up, all he could think about was learning more about Jesus. Who could help him in his newfound faith? Then he remembered a rumor about a group of Christians that had begun meeting and studying in the area. Ali knew who the leader was and sought him out.

The leader of this group – whom we shall call "T" – is an evangelist and church planter who works with OMS. For many months before this joyful day, T had been praying for persons of peace in Ali's community. Day after day, he and his small group of coworkers had cried out to the Lord for someone of reputation who could help the other souls trapped in the false religion of Islam to believe their message. Thus far, they had been met only with angry retorts and suspicious eyes whenever they tried to share with or befriend people in the town. So they had prayed harder, and they knew, by faith, that God was at work, even if they could not see a difference.

T had prayed again that morning, just a short time before he saw Ali coming to his house. T recognized Ali as the imam from the mosque. If anyone was going to order them to leave or give some sort of threat, it would be him. But Ali did not look angry or threatening, so T invited him in. Instead of trouble, the visit was an unbelievable blessing. Ali told him everything that had happened to him over the previous weeks, ending with his healing from Jesus just the day before.

Ali told T honestly that he needed to learn more about Jesus and how to follow him. The thought was positively staggering to T. Ali was an imam, a man of reputation and importance in the community. He had probably been inside the mosque leading worship and prayer when T and his team did their prayer walks through the town. T agreed to teach Ali, and they started lessons right away. Soon, the entire team embraced Ali as a new believer. Their friendship became important in the difficult days ahead when word spread that Ali had left the faith of Islam.

At this present time, Ali is a member of the evangelism and church planting team. He is an eager student who studies the Bible with great passion. Although he has been persecuted and rejected by many in his community, he has stayed strong in the faith. God has also used him, as a man of reputation, to be a powerful witness. He has given many people his personal testimony about the healing power of God that he experienced in his life.

God is at work even when we cannot see it. He is answering prayer even when we can see no evidence of it. T continued to pray faithfully and to sow seeds regardless of his circumstances; in God's time, T did reap a harvest of souls. So remember that even in the most difficult of mission fields, nothing is too hard for our God who is mighty to save.

Chief of Dobele

One by one, family by family, and village by village, the power of God is transforming Africa through thousands of faithful witnesses who have been equipped to share Jesus and who have caught the burden of searching for persons of peace. One such witness is Tabo, a present-day village church planter in the Central African Republic. He has ministered for several years with OMS.

Tabo has walked or biked many miles in rural areas to bring

the message of salvation to the African people. He often targets villages where there is no church and no Christian witness. Whenever he sets out on a mission of evangelism, he always makes sure he is covered in prayer, and he asks the Holy Spirit to lead him to persons of peace.

Not long ago, Tabo learned of a village called Dobele, which had no church. Dobele's inhabitants lived in fear of criminal activities caused by different gangs. These gangs were mainly made up of young men who robbed and intimidated everyone so often that no one felt safe.

Tabo's burden for Dobele grew, so he planned an evangelism trip. Soon after he arrived in the village, he met a woman who happened to be the local chief. Tabo introduced himself and was honest with her. He shared that he desired to see her village come to know Christ. He told her that he had been praying for the people and had brought a message to give to everyone about God and his Son, Jesus. Tabo told the chief that the people did not have to live in fear. Inwardly he was praying that the chief was a person of peace and that she would be receptive to his message.

Tabo did not know what the chief's response would be, but he knew that he had come in the name of Jesus and that he was covered in prayer. So he waited calmly to see whether he would be allowed to speak. Fortunately, he didn't have to wait long. The chief turned to her spokesperson and told him to quickly go and gather everyone together. She said that God had finally sent his servant to them and that they should all come to hear the good news.

Tabo's heart was filled with joy and relief as the young man took off running with the chief's command. Many people had been farming, tending goats, or washing clothes at the stream, but they all dropped what they were doing at the chief's summons and gathered around Tabo. Their faces looked eager to hear what he had to say.

Tabo preached the Word of God, and the Holy Spirit came in a wonderful way. After Tabo finished speaking, he asked for all to stand who desired to follow Jesus. More than eighty adults and thirty children stood to their feet. The chief was one of the first to stand, and she immediately allocated a piece of land on which they could build a church. She handed Tabo a stick and told him to mark off dimensions in the ground for the size of a church building they would need. Tabo could hardly believe that things were happening so fast. He was amazed that a church could be planted in just one day.

The chief certainly was a receptive person of peace and one who was effective because of her reputation in the village. She ordered the people to build the church without delay. The entire village worked together to clear the land and prepare the ground for the building to begin. While the church was being built, the chief gave Tabo lodging and food. Over the next several days, he baptized fifty-four people.

Over the next several months, Tabo watched the village transform through the power of Jesus and the teachings of his Word. The people feared the Lord and desired to live their lives to please him. The young boys and girls stopped being promiscuous, and the villagers stopped using drugs and alcohol and witchcraft. The criminal activity of the gangs also ceased, and many of the former gang members became followers of Jesus.

Instead of living in constant fear, the villagers of Dobele now live in joy and peace. The church members are enjoying God's protection, and they are serving him with zeal. Tabo continues to share Jesus with more and more villages in the Central African Republic, and God is continuing to transform them with his saving grace.

The chief of Dobele had been waiting for a long time to hear a message from God. She recognized Tabo as a true servant of the Lord and immediately wanted all of Dobele to hear his words. Not only did she accept Christ, but she also opened up a way for the message to continue to be preached by donating land for a church to be built. The chief provided the hospitality of lodging and food for Tabo just as Jesus described a person of peace should do. Through her influence as chief, she was able to gather the people together in order for them to hear the words of life that would forever change her village. She truly exemplifies a modern-day example of a person of peace who is a woman of reputation.

You may not live near a village that does not have a church, and you may never meet an African chief, but persons of peace who are longing to hear the good news live near you. Without a doubt, there are people in your own community who live in fear, and your own neighbors may have no peace in their hearts. You too can have a ministry just like Tabo's if you will only reach out.

Cemetery

The nation of Mozambique, in Africa, struggles with many challenges. It has one of the shortest life expectancy rates in the entire world, with an average lifespan of only forty years. Twelve percent of the people are HIV positive. With its lack of development, Mozambique has one of the world's lowest income levels, and most of its people live in severe poverty. Millions of its people believe in and rely on the satanic practices of witch doctors in their daily lives.

Currently, seventy thousand witch doctors are practicing in Mozambique. In many places, they are more popular and more trusted for desired results than the professionally trained doctors. When a client comes to a witch doctor, he goes through a ceremony to become inhabited by what people believe to be a spirit from the underworld. The people believe that this spirit has the power to heal the sick or to bring about a blessing or a curse, whichever the customer requests. These spirits may belong to a wild animal, a dead relative, a brave soldier, or even a biblical prophet.

The witch doctor receives instructions from the spirits on how to grant the requests. Based on what the spirits tell him, the witch doctor creates powders with various dried herbs, roots, insects, or bird parts, and instructs the customers to wear these powders in a pouch around their necks. Sometimes the instructions are much more extreme, however, and the witch doctor will tell the people to bathe in goat's blood or to lie flat on their backs while the witch doctor drips animal blood all over their bodies. Some customers even allow the witch doctor to make cuts all over their bodies with a razor blade.

Cemetery, an elderly witch doctor, lived in the town of Mocuba, Mozambique. He had practiced the art of "healing" as a witch doctor for many years and was quite famous in his town. His powers with the underworld were legendary. He was famous not only for healings, but also for sending curses of death upon a client's enemies. In fact, that is how he got his name: so many believed that his curses caused people to be buried in a cemetery that he was named after that place.

Today, Cemetery is a changed man. He is now in the business of helping to send people to heaven. The change in Cemetery began with a humble pastor named Antonio, who works in partnership with OMS. He has a great burden for the lost and is active in training and equipping others through OMS's village church-planting strategy.

One day, Antonio took some students to Cemetery's home. The students were nervous and wondered if he would try to put a curse on them. However, Antonio had been burdened for Cemetery for quite some time, and he believed the Holy Spirit was directing them to go to his house. They found Cemetery at home alone, and he allowed them to share the Gospel. This meeting was truly a divine appointment because God had already been working on his heart. Cemetery listened carefully to Antonio, and he readily accepted the Gospel message. He was completely ready to turn away from all the powers of darkness that had consumed his life for so long. He prayed so readily, in fact, that Antonio was suspicious of the authenticity of his conversion.

Antonio told Cemetery that he would come back in a week to begin teaching him more about being a follower of Jesus from God's Word. When Antonio returned, he was worried about how Cemetery would greet him, but his fears proved to be groundless. He found a joyful Cemetery sharing the Gospel with a group of people in his home. Cemetery was telling the people exactly what Antonio had told him the week before. He had burned all the items related to his craft, and in just a week of testifying, he had people in his home who were also ready to follow Jesus.

Cemetery was a true person of peace after all. His change was not an act, and he was already leading many others to Christ. His witness was effective in Mocuba because, as a witch doctor, he was a man of reputation. The fear and awe in which people held him as a witch doctor turned into love and joy once Cemetery began to witness to others about Jesus.

Cemetery had lost contact with his son years before because his son was afraid of his father's evil work with the spirits of death and destruction. But as soon as word reached him that his father had totally changed, his son came to see whether the stories were true. Cemetery had the joy of leading his son to Jesus as well.

Antonio and Cemetery are close friends now, and Antonio has trained and equipped Cemetery to be a village church planter. Cemetery decided to change his name, and today he is called Barnabe. His joy is complete because his son stayed with him to receive training in discipleship and equipping. Today, they work together as a beautiful team, sharing the Gospel and planting churches in rural Mozambique.

Barnabe demonstrates a ready person of peace who is successful because of his reputation. He immediately begins to refer others to Christ after receiving salvation. He didn't wait for training, and he didn't wait for more visits from Pastor Antonio. He happily began to share what he knew even before Antonio came back to his house with more messages from God's Word.

People from all around that region knew of Barnabe's reputation as a former witch doctor. They told stories of his power and exploits around cooking fires for decades. However, today he is still a man with a tremendous reputation, and people are still telling exciting stories about him. The difference is that the stories are all about the enormous change in his life. Now the stories bring glory to God and not to Satan. He was once a scary man of death and curses, and now he is known far and wide for his joy and laughter.

Antonio knew that Cemetery was steeped in sin, but that didn't stop him from making the effort and taking the time to go to his house. Antonio was faithful to be a witness, and once again, the Holy Spirit was able to do a mighty work. Then Antonio obeyed Jesus' instructions and continued to disciple Barnabe, equipping him to do the work of ministry. The revival continued onward with Barnabe leading his son to Christ and equipping him. May the line of changed lives never end.

Are you a part of a chain of changed lives like this? You can be if you engage in the search for persons of peace.

Chapter 5

A Person of Peace Is Connected

A person of peace is connected with many people that he can "refer" Jesus to in a variety of ways. When you make a referral, you send someone to another person for a consultation or to take further action. In the spiritual sense, when people receive salvation from Jesus, they become people of referral when they "send" (attempt to bring) their family, friends, and community to Jesus. These people of referral believe so strongly in their changed lives in Jesus that they want everyone they know to trust in him also.

New believers will naturally want to tell others all the good things they now know about the Son of God. In many contexts, however, this knowledge will be limited to their personal salvation story alone. As a new believer's friends, family, neighbors, and other connections hear about and desire to know more about Christ, a person of peace will then refer them to the messenger, who can provide greater knowledge and understanding of what it means to be a follower of Jesus Christ.

The following stories are examples of people of referral from the Bible, from pioneer missionaries, and from present-day witnesses. In the biblical examples, Jesus is the messenger, delivering the saving knowledge of himself. You will read amazing accounts of how God uses persons of peace to refer others to him. You will also see evidence of how God providentially puts strategic people of referral in the paths of ready witnesses.

Biblical Characters

Andrew

Andrew and his brother Simon were born in Bethsaida, a town on the north side of the Sea of Galilee. Because of its location by the water, both Andrew and Simon were fishermen, like their father. Andrew's faith must have been an integral part of his life, because when John the Baptist began his ministry, Andrew became one of John's disciples (John 1:35-40). As devout Jews, Andrew and Simon probably had many conversations about prophecy and the coming of the Messiah. They probably resented the Romans with their high taxes and control over the lives of the Jews. Both longed for the Messiah, who would make things right.

The day after John baptized Jesus, John was again at the Jordan River outside of Bethany with two of his disciples, one of whom was Andrew. When Jesus passed by, John said, *"Behold the Lamb of God!"* (John 1:36). Andrew and the other disciple followed Jesus to see for themselves who Jesus was and to talk to him. Jesus saw the two men following him and invited them to spend the day with him.

God had been working in Andrew's heart and had placed Andrew with John the Baptist at precisely the right moment for him to impact Andrew. It was not coincidence that brought Jesus back to the same location he was the day before. It was not coincidence that Andrew had been hungering for more information about the Messiah. It was not coincidence that Andrew could spend an entire day in Jesus' company so that he could learn about the Messiah's teaching. And it was not coincidence that God gifted Andrew with a heart for referring others to Jesus.

After the day he spent with Jesus, Andrew knew he was in the presence of the Messiah, and he knew that he wanted to follow Jesus. At that moment, Andrew became Jesus' first called disciple. Because Andrew's heart was impacted by the Holy Spirit to be a man of referral, the first thing he did was run home to tell his brother the news. Andrew shouted: *"We have found the Messiah"* (John 1:41).

The world was forever changed that day, the day that Andrew brought Simon to meet Jesus. Jesus took one look at Simon and changed his name to Cephas, or Peter, which means "the rock." Simon Peter would later go on to become one of the most powerful apostles for Jesus, thanks to his brother's referral.

Andrew brought others to Jesus through his gift of referral as well. When five thousand people came to hear Jesus preach, Andrew was concerned about how the people were to be fed, so that they could stay there, hear the truth from Jesus, and believe (John 6:5-11). He introduced Jesus to a boy who had five barley loaves and two fish. Through this action, Andrew helped expose thousands of people to a miracle and to the Savior of the world.

In another biblical example, Andrew also referred several Greeks to Jesus (John 12:20-21). Not only did Andrew refer Jews to Jesus, but he also introduced Gentiles to him. And Jesus responded to this inclusion by saying, *If anyone serves Me, let him follow me; and where I am, there My servant will be also. If anyone serves me, him My Father will honor* (John 12:26). Jesus was telling all the people listening to him that everyone who believes – both Jew and Gentile – would enter the kingdom of God.

Andrew is a great example of a person of peace. Through his faith and excitement, he left his job and his family to follow Jesus to the ends of the earth. Not only did he bring his brother to the Lord, but he also was instrumental in exposing both Greeks and thousands of other Jews to the person of Jesus.

Are you like Andrew? Do you have a burning passion to bring your family members to Jesus? Are you willing to run to them and tell them of the Savior, with the faith and excitement of Andrew? Look around your neighborhood and town. You can find people who need a messenger like Andrew to refer them to Jesus, the one they have been searching for all their lives. They are potential persons of peace who only need an introduction to the Master from someone who has met him. Whom are you referring to the Lord?

Matthew

Jesus had been performing many miracles and healing many people when he returned to Capernaum, a wealthy city on the Sea of Galilee. As he was walking along the streets of the city, he saw Matthew, sitting at his tax collector's booth. Jesus reached out to him and invited him to be his disciple. Matthew immediately left his booth and began to follow Jesus (Matthew 9:9-13).

As a tax collector, Matthew was an outcast from his Jewish neighbors because he was appointed by the Romans to collect taxes from the citizens and merchants. Tax collectors were paid from the commission they took from the taxes, and they often overcharged the people and then kept the profits for themselves. So when Jesus called Matthew to follow him, the other disciples were probably shocked and dismayed by this repulsive sinner. But through his choice, Jesus was demonstrating how we are to be his witnesses in this world.

What happens next is a wonderful example of how the Lord can use a person of peace to spread and multiply the Gospel. Not only did Matthew invite Jesus and his disciples into his home to have dinner with him, but he also invited many other tax collectors and sinners to meet Jesus (Matthew 9:10). The best evangelists are often the newest believers because they want to refer their unsaved friends to Jesus, like Matthew did.

The Pharisees objected to Jesus eating with these sinners and being in their homes. They asked the disciples why their teacher ate with such scum. When Jesus heard them, he said that it is the sick, not the healthy, who need a doctor (Matthew 9:12). Every society has people who are considered "the worst of the worst." They may be death-row prisoners, registered sex offenders, drug dealers who hang around outside our middle schools, prostitutes dressed provocatively on the corner, or drunk drivers who kill an innocent family in a head-on collision.

One day, God may send you a person of peace from the "the worst of the worst." How will you respond? Will you follow social customs and ignore these people on the fringes of society? Will you stay away in fear? Or will you purposefully try to build relationships with ones who put you at risk? Will you shun their neighborhoods and homes or enter in with the love of the Lord lighting your way?

Matthew had a clear idea of the cost of following Jesus. Several of the other disciples had a livelihood – such as fishing – to which they could always return when they needed the income. However, after Matthew left his lucrative position as a tax collector, he could never go back to it. But that knowledge did not stop Matthew from giving up everything to follow Jesus. I challenge you to search your own heart in the matter of income and security. Would you be willing to give up money or walk away from a job if that sacrifice is what following Jesus required of you? Would you leave home and all things familiar in the pursuit of sharing the good news with people who have not heard it?

God saw potential in Matthew as a record keeper too. He worked with detailed accounts every day as a tax collector. This skill and ability continued with him as a follower of Christ. He kept a detailed record of his time with Jesus. Matthew's book is the largest and most thorough record of all of the Gospels, and he did the most scholarly work in showing how Jesus fulfilled the Old Testament prophecies. Persons of peace in the modern world can also use their education, skills, and abilities for blessings in the kingdom of God. Don't let your potential go to waste. Discover how you can use your talents for the Lord.

Jesus also emphasized the importance of timing in his dealings with Matthew. Matthew was working when Jesus approached him. When Matthew left his job to follow Jesus, he became a man of referral to all the people who witnessed this dramatic conversion. What was it about Jesus that caused Matthew to drop everything and follow him? These people wanted to know the answers.

In the same way, we should witness to people who are working too. Don't hesitate to share the Gospel with your waitress, your doctor, your hairdresser, the insurance salesman, or the person working on your car. You can find persons of peace at all these places. God's timing for saving people's souls may be during their working hours, as it was with Matthew. You may be the person to bring that providential message to these working people. You should look for opportunities to do search-and-rescue work wherever you go.

The Samaritan Woman

When the northern kingdom of Israel fell to the Assyrians, many Jews were deported to Assyria. Foreigners were brought in to settle the land and keep the peace. These foreigners intermarried with the remaining Jews and created a mixed race – known as Samaritans – whom the Jews considered to be impure. Samaritans were unwelcome at the temple in Jerusalem, so they built their own at Mount Gerizim because many of them still loved God and wanted to worship him the only way they knew how. But their temple was destroyed 150 years before Jesus met the Samaritan woman at the well (John 4:4-42), so the Samaritan people were starved for the Word of God.

Most Jews avoided traveling through Samaria (located between Judea and Galilee) if they could, but Jesus was not one of them. His message was for everyone: men, women, children, Jews, and Gentiles – including Samaritans. Jesus and his disciples arrived in Sychar, a town in Samaria where Jacob's well was located. While the disciples went to purchase food, Jesus sat by the well.

At noon, a Samaritan woman came to draw water from the well. Because she did not have a good reputation in the town, she never came to the well when the other women were there. Jesus broke tradition by speaking to the woman and asked her for a drink of water. She responded with this question, *"How is it that You, being a Jew, ask a drink from me, a Samaritan woman?" For Jews have no dealings with Samaritans* (John 4:9).

Jesus responded by saying, *"If you knew the gift of God, and who it is who says to you, 'Give Me a drink,' you would have asked Him, and He would have given you living water"* (John 4:10).

With supernatural knowledge, Jesus then revealed to the woman that she had had five husbands and was now living with yet another man in a promiscuous relationship. Jesus also told her the truth about living water and that the day had come to worship God in spirit and in truth. A temple was not even necessary. Jesus concluded the conversation by revealing that he was the Messiah (John 4:26).

The whole dialog was astounding to the Samaritan woman. She was so excited that she forgot her own limitations of communicating with the other townspeople, and she ran back to Sychar as quickly as possible. She proclaimed the good news about the Messiah in the marketplace and encouraged the people to seek out Jesus at Jacob's well. She told the people that Jesus had proved himself by telling her everything she had ever done.

Several people came to the well that day and encouraged Jesus to stay for two more days. Because they heard the Word of God directly from Jesus, many Samaritans believed and became followers of Jesus. As a person of peace, the Samaritan woman at the well referred her whole town to Jesus. She didn't let her sin-wrecked past stop her from being a witness. She didn't let her blackened reputation hold her back. Her excitement was contagious, and her message was compelling.

Along with saving her soul, Jesus may have given the Samaritan woman a brand new start in life as well. With the excitement that she showed for the Word of God, she probably turned her life around to become a woman of faith in her town. Sometimes people with the worst backgrounds make wonderful persons of peace. The change in their lives is so dramatic that others can't help but notice the difference. People may come to hear your message simply out of curiosity and amazement at seeing the changed life of someone else. Conversions can open many doors for you to tell the message of the Gospel. The possibilities are endless, and the chain reactions can keep going and going.

The Demon-Possessed Man

In the region of the Gadarenes there lived a demon-possessed man (Mark 5:1-20). When Jesus crossed the Sea of Galilee to come to the region, the man was waiting for him when Jesus got off the boat. The people of the town had banished this poor man to the tombs because the demons made him so violent that the people feared for their lives. He had such strength that he could break apart the irons that the authorities used to chain him and shackle his feet.

Demons flee at the presence of Jesus and his Word, so when the man saw Jesus, the demons in him knew that Jesus would not let them remain. The man threw himself down at Jesus' feet, and the demons inside him screamed for Jesus not to interfere with them or to torture them. When Jesus asked them for their name, they said it was Legion (Mark 5:9). In the Roman army, a legion of men consisted of between three thousand and six thousand soldiers, so the man was possessed by many demons. Jesus didn't pay attention to the demons and commanded them to go. Then they begged him to send them into a large herd of pigs that was nearby. Jesus agreed, and the demons departed to the pigs. The pigs went mad, and the whole herd – about two thousand pigs – stampeded over a cliff and drowned.

The herdsmen who were watching the pigs ran to the village to tell everyone what had happened. Soon, the hills and roads were swarming with people who came to see the sight of the pigs in the Sea of Galilee. At this point, the story gets even stranger. Instead of being happy to see the demon-possessed man released from the demons, the people were upset over the loss of their pigs because they had just lost their village's investment. The life of one man in exchange for two thousand pigs was too high a price for the villagers to pay. They were also afraid of Jesus because they didn't understand his power, so they asked Jesus to leave their area. The conclusion of this story may be one of the saddest in the Bible, because the people chose pigs over Jesus. Jesus never pushed his way in anywhere and was always prepared to leave when he was not wanted.

The restored man, however, was so grateful for his healing and deliverance that he asked to go with Jesus first, rather than to go see his family. Jesus, in his wisdom and kindness, sent him back to his family and told him to tell others about the mercies of God. The man became a fantastic witness because he shared the good news not only with the people in his own town but with the people in ten other towns as well. He fulfilled his purpose and referred hundreds of others to the goodness and salvation of the Savior.

One day, God may lead you to someone in bondage to the Enemy when you are searching for persons of peace. Use your authority in Christ and set them free. We have power over demons in Jesus' name.

Historical Pioneer Missionaries

Do-Wai

Several aboriginal tribes lived in the mountains of Taiwan in the early 1900s. The Japanese controlled the island at that time and quickly deemed the aborigines to be cruel and barbaric. The Japanese called them pitfalls to the rest of the world and determined to conquer them or, at least, greatly subdue them. The Japanese wanted to contain the tribes to the mountains, so they quarantined the tribes and erected a highly electrified fence to keep them from the public.

One of the reasons that the Japanese went to the extreme of quarantining the tribes to the mountains was because several of the tribes were headhunters. The hunting parties usually struck in the dead of night or at a time when they could catch people out working in the fields, where they were isolated and away from any structures they could run to for safety. The victims' children were often caught too and brought back to the tribe, where they were then raised as full members of the tribe.

The hunting parties would decapitate their victims, boil the heads, and then hang them on a pole to dry. Sometimes the head was invited to become a part of the tribe and asked to watch over the people as a protector and communicator of their needs to the underworld. Often, the tribesmen wrote prayers on their arrows before going on a head-hunting mission. They believed that their prayers, going into the newly dead or dying person, would be transported by him to the spirits.

The Japanese saw no hope for change among these tribal peoples and thought that they would always be a danger to the rest of society. But the Japanese didn't count on the power of prayer and the power of God to cleanse and make new. Missionaries called by God to reach those very people were already on the island. These missionaries were searching for persons of peace who could take the good news to the various tribes and refer many more to the way of the cross.

The task was difficult because the Japanese did not allow the missionaries to go directly to the tribes in the quarantined area. They had to be patient, so they waited and prayed for God to send them a person of peace from one of the tribes. Finally, they met just such a dynamic young man by the name of Do-Wai, from the Tyal tribe. He had heard about Jesus through Chi-oang in the beginning of her ministry. (See chapter 3 for her story.)

Do-Wai opened his heart to the Gospel and believed. The truths brought him joy, filled him with holy boldness, and gave him an overwhelming desire to tell this truth to his people in the mountains. He went to the Japanese authorities and begged them to let him come off the mountain in order to go to Bible school. They flatly refused his request; however, this refusal did not stop Do-Wai, and he made his way down the mountain in secret. He lived in a room of a missionary's house for safety. Various missionaries and Christian teachers came regularly to teach him the Bible.

After two years of study, Do-Wai went back to his people and was soon able to send back word that he had thirty people ready to be baptized. His little church had been meeting secretly for two hours after midnight each week so that they would not be found by the police. The government hoped that the aborigines would eventually kill each other so that the problem of the hostile tribes would be solved that way. The growth of Christianity would hinder this plan, however, so the government tried to stop its spread throughout the tribes.

As more and more tribespeople converted to Christianity and asked to go off the mountain, the Japanese got angrier and angrier. For a while, the only thing the missionaries could do was smuggle Bibles up the mountain, but they had no further word from Do-Wai. Tensions grew worse until one day the missionaries received word that the Japanese had put Do-Wai in prison. Nothing more was heard from him for many years.

War then broke out between Japan and China, and the missionaries had to evacuate the island. Finally, in 1946, the first missionary returned to Taiwan. Miraculously he met Do-Wai. Everyone had assumed he was a martyr, but God had spared his life. Do-Wai had spent many years in prison and was persecuted terribly. The Japanese offered to free him many times if he would only renounce Christ, but Do-Wai stayed true and continued to refer others to the Savior. The record of his story estimates that Do-Wai led more than one thousand people into the kingdom.

Today, about 70 percent of the aboriginal peoples of Taiwan are Christian. This statistic shows the power of a small number of witnesses referring others to the Lord. One by one, these witnesses and persons of peace are building the kingdom of God and changing the world. Do-Wai continued to refer others to Christ no matter the cost, because he knew that nothing is more important in this world than getting out the message of the one true God and his Son, Jesus.

The missionaries did all they could by paving the way in preparation to receive this person of peace. They prayed for him even when they didn't know his name. Then they loved him and cared for him and welcomed him into their homes.

Finally, they spent a great amount of personal time with him in training and equipping him to be able to carry God's message. How much time are you willing to spend with a new believer? Sometimes the church simply dumps new people into a Sunday school class or a small home group and expects them to learn everything on their own. Jesus demonstrated a better way to make disciples by spending personal time with his followers. They were trained through both teaching and hands-on experiences. This is the kind of commitment to a new person of peace that God wants us to have.

Bodari Du-Dui

In the early 1900s, Bodari Du-Dui became a person of peace to his Ami tribe in the mountains of Taiwan, just as Do-Wai was a person of peace to his Tyal tribe. The Ami tribe was also a tribe of headhunters, and Bodari Du-Dui was in line to become its new chief. The Ami people lived in terrible darkness and were bound by the chains of demon worship and blood sacrifices. Revenge killings were the norm, as were witches and satanic ceremonies. Bodari's father had been killed by a rival tribe, so his grandfather – the current chief – trained him to be chief and to seek his first revenge killing whenever he had the opportunity.

While other Ami children went to school, Bodari was becoming skilled in the use of all the tribal weapons. His grandfather saw no use for academics when the knowledge of war and leadership were what Bodari would need most. His grandfather passed down the traditions of the tribe. He directed the raids and attacks on other tribes. He executed justice and administered punishments. He was the ultimate judge over all Ami matters and was to be obeyed without question. His grandson, though, was strong willed and an independent thinker.

Bodari Du-Dui had lots of questions, and his questions were an aggravation to his grandfather:

- Is it wrong to kill?

- What is the meaning of our religion?

- Why do we sacrifice to demons?

- Why are witches called when someone dies?

- Why are new babies offered up to evil spirits?

- Why must we kill a four-footed beast every time a head is brought home?

- How do we know our religion is right?

Bodari was becoming skeptical and was not satisfied with the evasive answers he received from his grandfather and the elders. His questions went on and on as he grew to be a teenager and trained to become chief. He also felt a longing in his heart to know more and to understand the religion of his people. Something did not feel right in his soul. Even from childhood, he was seeking the truth about God, and God knew his every thought.

Finally, when Bodari was an older teen, his grandfather allowed his great uncle – who had been educated by the Japanese – to teach him the rudiments of education. This knowledge awakened even more his thirst for answers. After four years of study, he desired to go further, so he asked his grandfather for permission to enroll in a teacher's training course. This kind of request was typically denied for tribal people, but God had his hand on the future of Bodari and miraculously provided a way through his grandfather.

His grandfather was able to get Bodari into a school because of family connections with Japanese leaders in that area. Nearing the end of his studies, at the age of twenty-five, the Lord sent many people to witness in different ways to Bodari Du-Dui. In preparing his heart, the Lord exposed him to Christians who sang and shared their testimonies on the streets. Bodari looked at their joyful faces and was drawn to them. He wanted joy like that too. He wondered if those people knew the answers to the questions that had plagued him all the years of his life. The Holy Spirit was preparing Bodari's heart for his encounter with a witness who was searching for persons of peace.

This witness was a young man named Komod-Kabala. Their meeting may have been unexpected to them both, but it was planned by the Lord. Komod-Kabala was of royal birth (like Bodari Du-Dui), was from a different tribe, and was also in a teacher's training course. As the son of a chief, his family connections had provided a way for his schooling as well. Their common lineage and background experiences drew them together immediately as friends.

Komod-Kabala shared his testimony and the plan of salvation with Bodari Du-Dui, and Bodari was convinced even more that he was hearing the truth. He went with Komod-Kabala to church, and there he met a Japanese missionary named Fujio Abe, who answered all the questions of his heart. They talked for hours, and Pastor Fujio assured Bodari that salvation and forgiveness were available no matter what his past had been. History records that Bodari knelt there that night and sought the Lord for a long time. He confessed his sins and repented until he had poured out everything in his heart to God. Finally, feeling like the sun had burst into his soul, he knew he was forgiven. He finally had true joy and the peace he had longed for since childhood.

In the newness of his salvation, Bodari Du-Dui would break out in singing and dancing. Other students thought he had lost his mind. But there was one thing he knew he had to do as soon as possible. He had a new Christian family now, but he still loved his people. They were his first family, and the greatest desire of his heart was to learn the Bible well enough that he could go and tell them the wonderful truths of the Word. Bodari truly had the heart of a person of peace who longed to refer others to Jesus. He took his responsibility seriously and spent the rest of his life as a leader to his people. He was not the leader that his grandfather had envisioned, but he became a dynamic preacher who was the first to show the way of Christ to his Ami tribe.

As God brings persons of peace for you to lead to Christ, one of the first questions you should ask them is "Who can you tell your good news to?" Find out their connections to other people and make immediate plans for helping them become a bridge to others. In the past, believers thought that a new Christian had to be taught and discipled for a long time before engaging in any kind of ministry. This idea is not based on biblical principles. Over and over in the Gospels and in the book of Acts, we see that new converts were immediately racing to tell their families and townspeople what had just happened to them so that the people could see their joy.

When you find a new person of peace and lead them to Christ, you should begin involving them in ministry with you. Help them to share their testimony of salvation and involve them in opportunities to share it. This experience will also help them to grow in their faith. Most importantly, they may be able to refer you to many other receptive hearts.

Chief Ga Tzao Mang

Ga Tzao Mang was also the chief of an Ami tribe in a section of the mountains of Taiwan. Ga Tzao was famous for his ability to drink, which he had been doing since he was a child as encouraged by the occult practices of his tribe. He could drink far more than the average person, and he had incredible arrogance in this ability. As chief, Ga Tzao was invited to numerous meetings and feasts, and these gatherings always included heavy drinking by all the participants, so he had endless opportunities to show off his skill.

The only thing Ga Tzao loved more than drinking was his occult following. He had a convoy of witches and witchdoctors that accompanied him wherever he went. He even married a well-known witch. The top witch doctor of the tribe was his right-hand man, who used his sorcery to advise the chief on all tribal matters. The witch doctor was the mediator for the tribe, and he sought the help of demons for drought, disease, successful hunts, and victories in war. To that end, the tribe held numerous ceremonies to honor and seek the help of demons. These ceremonies always included drunkenness as well.

For more than ten years, Ga Tzao indulged in fermented drinks and every sort of debauchery in the world of the occult. But one night, as the witch doctor was receiving communications from an evil spirit, the chief continued to drink all night. For the first time, he almost drank himself to death, and that was his wake-up call. Even though Ga Tzao bragged about his drinking and his high connections to the underworld, he feared death. He did not want to die, so he was determined never to drink so much again. However, his lifestyle and responsibilities as chief demanded he attend all these meetings, ceremonies, and feasts, which centered on drinking. He carried his fear of death inside as a well-kept secret.

Meanwhile, a Christian witness, Oi Yoshie, had been praying for persons of peace. She was the Japanese wife to Komod Kabala, who led Bodari Du-Dui to the Lord. This husband-wife team went to the first Bible school of OMS in Tokyo. Together they agreed to return to Taiwan as missionaries to the unreached tribal peoples in the mountains.

Ga Tzao first encountered Oi Yoshie in the town of Shuilien, which was located close to the mountains. She and her husband had settled there to be close to the tribal peoples. Her face radiated joy and peace. Ga Tzao watched her from a distance and was envious. Although he was ruler over many people and had much influence in his tribe, he never felt the sense of peace that appeared to radiate from this woman. He asked other people about her, and they all testified to her kindness and happiness. Many of these people envied her too and wanted to know why she was so different.

Whenever Ga Tzao met her, Oi Yoshie was always gracious and polite. After each meeting, the chief felt sadder and more dissatisfied with his own life. Ga Tzao didn't know it, but the lady had begun to pray for him. She was praying behind the scenes that God would convict his heart and draw him to the Lord.

The chief eventually learned the story about the woman and her husband. He discovered that Komod Kabala, who was the son of a fellow chief, had rejected the religion of his people. This man claimed to worship one great and true God. He had even left Taiwan to go to Japan for schooling and so met Oi Yoshie. They both worshiped this God, and they had been teaching their religion, which they called the good news, to his own people.

The chief was disturbed, confused, and interested all at the same time. On the one hand, he was upset about how these missionaries dared to dispute his traditions and make a mockery of the occult and the witch doctors. On the other hand, he was also wondering about whether this good news could help make him feel happy and not drink so much.

One night, in his confusion, the chief could not sleep. He wanted answers, and he could wait no longer. The chief made his way, alone, back to the town of Shuilien. He went to the missionaries' home and waited in front of their house for dawn to come. When Oi Yoshie awoke, she found this great chief standing at her door. Gracious as always, she let him in and invited him to eat breakfast.

"Thank you," the chief said, "but I have really come to get the medicine which will give a man peace and help him stop drinking."

The lady smiled because she knew the Lord was answering her prayers. When breakfast was ready, she told the chief that they must thank God for the food.

"How can she pray with no witch doctor here?" he thought to himself.

As soon as the meal was over, he asked her again for the medicine that would give him peace and help him stop drinking. But instead of answering, Oi Yoshie went to another room and brought back a book. She told him that if he would believe the truth in this book, he would find peace and be able to stop his drinking. She went on to explain the way of salvation. Right then and there, Chief Ga Tzao Mang became a Christian. The Lord answered the woman's prayers, and a new person of peace came to know the Lord.

In his happiness, the chief began to shout "I have found him!" He was also completely delivered from alcoholism from that day on.

That night, the Lord sent Ga Tzao a vision. He saw an elderly man wearing a white robe. He told the chief that now he must go and tell all his people the message of the one true God. From that day on, Ga Tzao went everywhere referring people to the Lord and telling them the good news. His changed life began a stream of salvation through the lives of many people in the mountains of Taiwan. The first people he went to were his occult followers, the witches and witch doctors. Many of them believed in the one true God and also began referring the truth to others. The highest-ranking witch of his tribe became a believer and was a tremendous influence as well.

We can learn so much from Oi Yoshie. Do you radiate peace and joy as she did in this story? Are people attracted to you and want to know why you are different? Do you pray regularly for people you meet, as she did for the chief after she met him? To help you continue to pray for lost people in your life, keep a prayer list as a regular reminder and so that you can refer to these names as the Holy Spirit prompts you to pray for them.

Chief Ga Tzao Mang's first act of obedience as a new believer was to go to his closest friends and associates, the witches and witch doctors, and point them to the Savior. He was even commissioned by the Lord through a vision on the same day he was converted. God did not want to waste any time in using Ga Tzao as a mighty person who could refer so many more to the Lord.

Warasa Wange

In the 1900s, approximately five hundred thousand Gedeo, an ethnic people, lived in the southern and central part of Ethiopia. The Gedeo people knew there was a great and benevolent God, whom they called Magano. Few people ever prayed to him, however, because they felt separated from him because of their sins. They did not feel they were close enough to Magano to ask him anything or to receive his favor, and they didn't know how to please him. So the Gedeo spent all their time trying to appease an evil being called Sheit'an.

Warasa Wange was born into this group of people in the early 1900s. He lived near a town called Dilla, which was on the edge of the tribal lands. His people were mainly coffee growers and lived as subsistence farmers from crop to crop, season to season. Warasa Wange was one of the few Gedeo people who sought knowledge of and fellowship with Magano. He prayed over and over for Magano to reveal himself to his people. One special day, that prayer was answered with a vision.

In the vision, Warasa Wange saw two strangers with white

skin. They were putting up small shelters under a large syca-more tree. Warasa recognized that tree. He knew it was located on the outskirts of his hometown. Another vision came, and this one showed the men building more permanent structures. Soon these buildings were everywhere on the hillside. They were strange looking to Warasa because the roofs were made of something shiny. (He had experienced only grass roofs in the villages.) Suddenly Warasa heard a voice say, "These men will bring you a message from Magano, whom you seek. Wait for them."

In the final scene of his vision, Warasa saw himself take the center pole from his house and carry it out to the white strangers. He set it on the ground next to the men. In Gedeo symbolism, the center pole from your house represents your life. So Warasa understood that in the future, his entire life and identity would involve those men and the message they would bring him about Magano.

Years went by, and nothing happened. However, soothsayers among his people also testified that strangers were coming with a message from Magano. Warasa continued to wait patiently and watch. Finally, after eight years, two pioneer missionaries – Albert Brant from Canada, and his ministry partner, Glen Cain – arrived on the border of Gedeo land in an old, beat-up truck. They had been praying and preparing for quite some time. Their calling from the Lord was to the Gedeo people.

In the 1940s, these two men desired to set up their mission work right in the middle of Gedeo land. However, because of political unrest at that time, the government would permit them to set up their camp only on the edge of Gedeo land, in the town of Dilla. Although the men were disappointed that they had to live on the edge of the tribal lands, they were still in good spirits and full of faith that God would send them persons of peace. So they drove toward Dilla in search of a location that would provide shade for their camp.

On the edge of town, the two men saw the same huge sycamore tree that Warasa had seen in his vision. It was a God-ordained, perfect place for the men to put up their tents and for the message of salvation and reconciliation to reach the Gedeo people.

Warasa heard the sound of the noisy old truck pulling up, and the rest, as you can imagine, is heralded in the mission history books. God heard the cries of Warasa and was answering his prayers. Warasa was a person of peace who proved to be an awesome man of referral to the rest of his people. He grew in faith and in relationship with the witnesses God had sent, and together they worked in sharing the good news for many decades. Today, the majority of Gedeo people are Christians. Nearly every Gedeo individual has heard the Gospel message of how to be reconciled with Magano, the one true God.

The missionaries to Ethiopia were faithful to hear and answer God's call to go. Then God used circumstances through the opening and shutting of doors to get them to just the right place at just the right time to lead them to Warasa, God's chosen person of peace. The Bible says in John 10:27: *"My sheep hear My voice, and I know them, and they follow Me."* Are you following close enough to the Lord to hear his voice? Can he direct you to a person of peace that he has prepared to bring your way? Can he trust you to be obedient to go after hearing his call?

Pu Chan

The Wa – which means "mountaineer" – was a large group of people who lived in the mountains of Burma (now Myanmar) and southwest China in the early 1900s. The Wa were in severe bondage to evil spirits who demanded human sacrifice in return for a good crop, so head-hunting parties went out in search of victims before every new season. Their heads were planted in the fields along with the farmer's seeds in the belief that the people would be rewarded with a bountiful harvest. Other heads were hung on three-pronged poles surrounding the villages to keep the people living in fear. A common saying among the witch doctors was: "There is no sight as beautiful as the three-pronged fork."

The evil spirits also demanded that the people sacrifice three thousand cows each year for varied reasons, which kept the people in severe poverty. Children in the villages often had no clothes, and the people were starving because the evil spirits were demanding their food and possessions as sacrifices. The evil spirits also demanded revenge killings, even if the deaths were accidental. The back-and-forth revenge killings often went on for generations. The bloodlust was endless, and the people lived in fear because of these constant demands. Life was cheap.

But God was also at work among the Wa. Occasionally, he would raise up a prophet, and that person would tell them that head-hunting and killing were wrong. The prophets would beg the people to stop trying to please the evil spirits and to break away from them. The Wa knew that there was one true God, and in their language he was called Siyeh. They knew that Siyeh had created all things. But the Wa people didn't know what Siyeh wanted them to do. They had lost all knowledge of him through the centuries. Wa legend said that the knowledge of Siyeh had been given to their forefathers in a book, but the book and all knowledge about God had been lost long ago.

Pu Chan was one of those prophets. He was born in the 1880s, and he had been a seeker after Siyeh for nearly all his life. Pu Chan desired more than anything to serve Siyeh and to please him, so he did his best to point others to Siyeh as well. Pu Chan's heart would grieve when the people brought new heads into the village because he knew inside that God was displeased. He asked God over and over again to show his people how to please him.

One day, Pu Chan heard a voice that said, "I will send a white brother with a copy of the lost book. This book will contain my message to your people." Pu Chan was so excited that he preached about Siyeh even more fervently to the people in his area. He was afraid that if this white brother came and heard of their evil deeds, he would turn back, and the Wa would never get to have the lost book restored to them. Pu Chan was so successful with his preaching that he convinced the Wa in that territory to stop head-hunting.

One day, God spoke to Pu Chan again. This time, God told him to saddle a pony. He told him that the pony would lead his disciples to the white brother who was near. By faith, Pu Chan got a pony ready and told some of his disciples to follow that pony wherever it went. He told them that the pony would lead them to the white brother with the lost book and that the man could use the pony to ride back on. In the Wa culture, the pony would indicate that the people considered the man an important guest.

While Pu Chan was still speaking, the pony started walking, so Pu Chan quickly shouted for the men to follow it. The pony led the disciples over two hundred miles, up and down mountain trails. Finally, the pony went down into the city of Kengtung, walked right into the gate of a missionary's home, headed straight for the well, and stopped. The disciples looked all around, but they could not see anyone. Then the men heard sounds down in the well. They looked down, and looking up at them were two blue eyes and a white face. The face belonged to pioneer missionary William Marcus Young. He welcomed the disciples and climbed out of the well that he had been digging. He was covered in dirt.

"Have you brought us a book about God?" one of the men

asked cautiously. What a fantastic question for a missionary. Young nodded and looked at them curiously. He somehow knew he was witnessing a miracle. Then the Wa men were overcome with emotion and fell at his feet. One after another, they told him all about Pu Chan and the assignment that had led them there. They told him that the pony was for him and asked him to come back with them because the people were waiting to hear about the one true God.

William Marcus told them that he could not leave right then because thousands of Lahu people were coming for teaching every day. He was in the midst of a great revival with the Lahu tribe. (See the section called "Men of the Lahu Tribe" in chapter 3.) However, Young happily arranged for the men to stay with him, and he began to teach them so that they could take the message back to their people. William Marcus Young gave the men this promise: "If I can't get to you, my sons will get to you. If my sons can't get to you, my grandsons will get to you. If my grandsons can't get to you, my great-grandsons will get to you."

Not only did Young teach the Wa disciples, but he also arranged for some of his assistants to go back with the men as well. Over the next several years, constant trips back and forth were arranged among the missionaries, teachers, and Wa people for teaching and equipping in the Word of God. Pu Chan was one of those who became a primary teacher of the truth to the Wa people. How grateful they were to learn that God forgave their sins and that he required no more sacrifice because of the one pure and perfect sacrificial death of God's Son, Jesus.

Young's son Vincent became a missionary like his father and translated the Bible into the Wa language. But for many years, Bibles were so rare and precious that pastors would carefully wrap them in plastic bags and bury them in the ground for safety and security after each use. The Wa considered the Bible to be their most precious possession. The revival continued for many decades. Today, approximately 15 percent of all the Wa people are evangelical Christians, and in 2012, a brand new Bible translation was completed in the Wa language.

Jeremiah 29:13 says, *And you will seek Me and find Me, when you search for Me with all your heart.* Pu Chan is an example of this promise being fulfilled. He earnestly sought the Lord for himself and for his people. As a true person of peace and a man of referral, he desired the reconciliation of his people to God just as much as he wanted it for himself. God performed an incredible miracle with a pony in order to answer Pu Chan's prayer.

God's witness, William Marcus Young, was ready to teach and equip disciples so that they could spread the message. In just a short amount of time, God's Word saved ten thousand Wa and equipped other persons of peace and missionaries to go farther into Burma and southwestern China. And the news is still spreading today. The stream is still flowing.

Persons of peace just as earnest as Pu Chan may live near you. They may be crying out to God even though they do not know him yet. They too may be bound in the darkness of sin, and they too may be living in fear. Will you search for them? Will you be the one with the message in the book of all books that reaches them?

Present-Day Witnesses

Mr. Toi

Caodaism is a religion mainly practiced in Southeast Asia. It was founded in 1926, and today has more than seven million adherents in many different countries. The religion teaches that there have been three periods of revelation in which individuals such as Buddha, Mohammad, and Jesus were appointed by God to give the world more spiritual understanding. Over time, the message from these spiritual leaders was corrupted, resulting in disharmony and confusion among the peoples of the earth. The founder of Caodaism claimed to have the final revelation of God and also claimed to have received his teachings from a spirit that was actually God. This spirit supposedly spoke to him on many occasions over several years.

The religion contains beliefs from every major religion of the world and promotes itself as the final universal religion that unites and brings peace to everyone. Caodaism encourages its followers to continue to receive guidance and direction from spirits, just as its founder did. The followers believe that these spirits are wise beings from another dimension, when in actuality they are quite likely demons posing as these benign spirits.

Followers of Caodaism regularly engage mediums who channel spirits. The mediums use instruments, such as Ouija boards, to receive instructions and answer questions. Sometimes, during séances, the medium uses a small table that tips in one direction or another. Then the table legs make tapping noises on the floor; the number of taps indicates the answer received. Mediums also utilize pens that are suspended in the air and write messages by spirits to answer questions from the participants.

Missionaries from OMS deal with followers of Caodaism regularly in Southeast Asia. Mr. Toi – whose name, location, and family information have been changed to keep them safe – is a person of peace that several OMS missionaries encountered. Mr. Toi was a practicing Caodaist who had a Christian daughter. He had a heart disorder and was admitted to the hospital at 6:00 a.m. one day. He died at the hospital at 5:00 a.m. the following day. After being pronounced dead by the doctor, his body was transferred to his home, as is customary, so his family could prepare it for burial. His body would soon receive a preservative injection to prevent decomposition.

Mr. Toi's daughter, Luan, was seventeen at the time and

was at work when she received news of her father's death. Luan was the only Christian in the family. Mr. Toi and all the other family members practiced Caodaism fervently and implacably disapproved of Luan's conversion. Luan could not get home until 8:00 a.m. As soon as she got home, her mother sent her to the market to buy funeral supplies, and she was gone for several hours. Her family sent her on errands two more times until she tearfully asked to be allowed to spend some time with her father in prayer. Her mother allowed her to do this.

So Luan sat by her father's body, held his hand, and began to pray. Luan wept before the Lord. So many times she had asked God for her family's salvation. And now she was heartbroken because her father had died without ever receiving Christ. Suddenly, she began to pray and ask God to restore him to life so that he could be saved. She refused to accept that this was the end and that he was lost forever.

After several minutes, she felt his hand move in her hand. Luan's eyes sprang open, and she saw her father's eyes also begin to open. A photographer had come to take pictures, which is another common custom, and he saw the miracle happen and ran from the house in terror. Luan cried for her mother to come and see.

Quickly the family transferred Mr. Toi to another hospital. Slowly he was able to speak and then to eat, until he was fully recovered and released from the hospital after only four days. Luan happily invited her church leaders to visit her father and to see for themselves the answer to her prayers. Everyone was joyful, and that evening the church leaders and Luan took the opportunity to witness to the family of the power and glory of God. This time her family really listened.

Not only did God bring back Luan's father from the dead, but he also answered her prayers. Through this miracle, Mr. Toi, his wife, and seven other relatives came to know Christ.

Today, their full allegiance is to the Lord, and their belief in mediums and spirits has been replaced with a full commitment to the guidance they receive from God's Word.

Mr. Toi is so grateful to have received a second chance in life that he joyfully shares his story of resurrection with everyone who will listen. As a person of peace, he is constantly referring his friends and neighbors to hear the message of Jesus. He even speaks to strangers in the marketplace about his conversion and the power of God.

Yes, God is still raising the dead in this present day. We should be so thankful for the faith of Luan, who is just a young Christian. May our faith imitate hers, and may we see God's power manifested in beautiful ways for the sake of the lost. Nothing is too hard for our God, and we shouldn't be afraid to ask him for even those things that seem humanly impossible.

Lance

Not long ago, the Lord began to speak to two couples: Paul and Dawn Cox (former OMS missionaries) and Christian and Robin MacKinnon (OMS special assignment missionaries). Both couples love children and are gifted parents. They knew that God was challenging them to minister to hurting children, so they took training courses to transform their homes into safe places for children, through a national organization called Safe Families for Children. Safe Families for Children is a network of individuals and churches that provide care and support for children whose families are in crisis.

Early in their ministry with Safe Families for Children, the organization asked Paul and Dawn to care for two children who were living in an old hotel with their dad. The facility was a run-down, pay-by-the-week lodge that was home to lots of people who were all struggling in life. The children loved their dad and wanted to stay together as a family, but he was having difficulty providing for them.

As Paul and Dawn's relationship grew with the children, they also had opportunities to meet the children's dad, a man named Lance. Lance was trying to hold down a low-paying job while struggling with depression. He felt like he couldn't get a break. He was finding it difficult to make ends meet, but he cared for his children and did not want to lose them. He also suffered from past addictions. The children's mother was not in the picture at all.

The family needed help with the basics of life, so Paul and Dawn began bringing them nutritious food. They tutored the children with schoolwork and provided counseling and encouragement. Naturally, they also shared Jesus with the family as God gave them opportunities. Lance would listen and sometimes ask searching questions, and the Coxes began to hope that he might be a person of peace for the Lord. But Lance put off making a commitment to Christ. However, Paul and Dawn continued to sow seeds faithfully and to do all they could to stabilize life for the children.

Time went on and their relationships grew. One day, Lance commented, "You guys bring us so much. We can't even eat it all. I feel bad because all around me in this hotel there are so many suffering people. There are others here who do not have enough to eat. Not only that, but there are a lot of people who could be helped through hearing about all you guys are telling me about Jesus."

Paul responded immediately that he would love to help the other people and asked Lance if he had any ideas. In fact, Lance did. He went to the manager of the hotel and asked if they could begin to have an open gathering time in the old hotel lobby with free food provided. The manager agreed, and a new ministry began.

Every week, the two couples cooked and brought a meal for all the residents. It was a casual fellowship time and a way to demonstrate God's love in action. More and more people began to come. The couples met many who struggled with alcoholism and drugs and whose lonely eyes held looks of desperation. They met abuse victims and young mothers who were trying to get free from domestic violence situations. Several heavily made-up girls in short skirts came in looking both cautious and curious. The couples soon learned that they were trapped in the sex industry and desperately wanted out.

The Coxes and MacKinnons met and loved many people who had been beaten down through their life experiences. The old couches were worn and the carpet was threadbare, but the atmosphere in that hotel lobby was full of warmth and words of hope. The couples sowed seeds of the Gospel to people who had no other Christian witness in their lives. Some had never heard the Gospel. One by one, lives were turned around through their witness and encouragement.

Then some of the new Christians asked the couples to bring them additional teaching and discipleship time. So a new element was added to the mealtime: they began to have church. Additional volunteers added music and testimonies, and God moved even more.

Paul kept expecting Lance to give his heart to Christ. After all, it was his idea for the food and fellowship time in the lobby that birthed all the other ministry opportunities. Because Lance made the arrangements with the manager of the hotel, the couples were able to reach so many more people with the Gospel.

But still Lance resisted, and finally he and his children moved on to another place in hopes of a better life in another town. Paul realizes now that even though Lance never accepted Christ during that time, God still used him as a person of peace as he referred people to the Coxes and the MacKinnons, who then shared Jesus with them. Through Lance, the Holy Spirit opened doors to the Gospel so that many more could hear and believe. He arranged the meetings where many people were loved and lives were changed.

In the process of sowing your seed, you may encounter similar circumstances. Witnessing to one person may open doors to many more opportunities, even when the person with whom you started never responds in faith. But God is at work through it all. He will find a way to reconcile persons of peace to himself, even by using unbelievers to make the connections.

Alieshy

Rich Yoder and his wife, Anita, are present-day missionaries with OMS. They serve the Lord by doing evangelism and church planting in a nation that cannot be identified because of security reasons. Although their ministry must keep a low profile, a house-church planting movement is advancing like a mighty rushing river across that country.

Christians in this nation set yearly goals of what they would like to see happen in their country regarding evangelism and church planting. In 2012, not only were all of their goals met, but they were also wildly surpassed. In 2012, they desired to see 3,980 people trained to search for persons of peace and begin house churches. By the end of that year, they had tripled that goal with more than 14,000 people trained. They set a goal of having 11 training centers for these new recruits. In actuality, they opened 152 training centers. They set a huge goal of more than 7,000 new house churches in 2012, and that goal was reached and nearly doubled by 2013. Truly, the Holy Spirit is being poured out in this country.

In Rich's sphere of influence, he met a young man named Alieshy, who became a part of this great movement for the Lord as a person of peace and a man of referral in his community.

Alieshy was eighteen years old when his uncle became a Christian. His uncle was the first Christian in the family, and his conversion shocked everyone because this man had lived a rough life and was known for his high consumption of alcohol each day. The family members became more and more amazed as they saw the changes in his life. He shared the Gospel with everyone at a family gathering, but no one accepted Christ that night. Everyone had a wait-and-see attitude about him, just waiting to see how long it would be before he fell off the wagon and went back to his old ways.

One day, Alieshy was at his grandmother's house, and he found a Bible that his uncle had left there. He gingerly picked it up. The laws in this country are so severe that Alieshy had never before held a Bible in his hands. Holding that book was like holding a precious jewel. He could not help but begin to read it. Over the next several days, he hungrily devoured the Bible, and the Holy Spirit began to work in his heart.

After Alieshy found the Bible, his uncle invited him to church to attend an evangelistic outreach event. That night, he heard the Gospel again, but he still did not have the courage to pray in front of all the people. However, when he was alone on the road going home, he could wait no longer, and he prayed to the Lord for salvation. "I was suddenly so filled with joy it was unbelievable," Alieshy always tells people. "I couldn't even understand it, but a joy came over me like nothing I have ever experienced."

His uncle was happy to hear the news, and they began to go to church together. Soon, a Christian brother from the church took Alieshy under his wing and began to disciple and mentor him in the faith. Every week, this brother would come to his house for Bible study, prayer, encouragement, and training to do evangelism. Alieshy testified that the personal time with this brother greatly helped to transform his life so that he could be used for the Master. When he seemed ready, his mentor encouraged Alieshy to begin to disciple someone else. This concept was scary and new for Alieshy, but he wanted to try it.

"Here I am, Lord; send me." Alieshy prayed these words out loud while his heart was wondering if he could really be a mentor to someone else. He was afraid, but he also wanted to do God's will. With accountability and weekly coaching from his mentor, Alieshy began a house church. He started with one other family. Their relationship with the Lord and with each other got stronger as they prayed together and studied God's Word. They worked hard inviting more people to come to the meetings. Alieshy followed the pattern of his church and mentor as he put older Christians with younger Christians for discipleship and training. He became a man of referral as he brought more and more people to the knowledge of the Lord through the work of the Holy Spirit.

Right in front of Alieshy's eyes, the Holy Spirit birthed a beautiful chain reaction in that small house church and across the entire nation. Believers invite new people to a house group meeting; the older believers disciple and train the new believers; before long, the new believers are reaching out and training other people; and the whole cycle repeats itself.

In every house church, the believers cover all their needs and requests in prayer every week. They make vigorous plans to spread the Gospel, and they even meet for prayer walks in various areas farther out from the cities. They ask God for new house churches every seven kilometers. God is giving them the desires of their hearts.

Alieshy has followed the Lord for more than twenty years now, and he has seen many miracles. Many people have been delivered out of spiritism, demon possession, and bondages to alcohol and sexual sin. The believers particularly target dark places that need the light of the Gospel, and again and again they have seen God's light and joy come into that darkness in powerful ways.

Alieshy is a great example of a new Christian who was mentored well. He was taught from the beginning that he had a responsibility to share his faith and testimony with others. Therefore, he began to search for additional persons of peace soon after his own conversion. He still works tirelessly in the pursuit of lost souls. He is a vision caster for others, inspiring them to reach their friends and family with the Gospel message. He clearly sees converts as bridges to other lost souls.

We should thank God for the uncle who was the first to share the Gospel with Alieshy and take him to church. We should also thank God for the Christian brother who discipled and trained him to search for the lost. That brother equipped him to begin a house church so that he could equip others to do the same. What appears to our eyes to be just one person reaching out to another person as a slow trickle, can really be in God's eyes a stream of people over a period of time growing into a mighty rushing river as we follow Jesus' principles of evangelism.

Saroz

Jim Hogrefe, veteran missionary and former director of church-planting movements for all fields of OMS, has ministered in dozens of nations, but extensively in India. He shared the account of the "Man on the Train" section in chapter 3, about a young couple named Anil and Samita in rural India. Jim has been their friend and church-planting coach for many years. They had a divine appointment with a stranger on a train that led to the salvation of an entire household, as well as many individuals in a community.

Anil and Samita are young and don't have much in the way of material possessions. But as children of God, they are rich in what truly matters the most: faith in the Lord. God continues to use them to find persons of peace in northern India, and this story is about another one of their encounters.

One morning, Samita was at the market of a larger village named G-pur. She often walked there because the choices of fruits and vegetables were more varied than in her own small village. She hoped to finish shopping and return home before noon because the day was already hot. As she walked home on the dusty road, she made casual conversation with a woman named Saroz. Saroz was wearing a worn and faded blue sari, and Samita wondered if she had a difficult life.

Saroz was a few years older than Samita and lived in a nearby town with her parents, brother, his wife, and their children. Extended families often live together under one roof in this part of the world. Samita told Saroz about her husband, Anil, and their faith in Jesus Christ. Saroz was interested and invited Anil to come to her house and tell her more about Jesus. Samita didn't hesitate. She pulled out her mobile phone and called her husband right away. Anil made arrangements to visit Saroz that day.

In the afternoon, Anil rode his bicycle into town, found the narrow alley, and walked his bicycle down the alley until he reached Saroz's home. He called into the house, as is customary, and Saroz hurried to the door to welcome him. As he entered the tiny room, he noticed the sparse furnishings. She closed the door, and there was only one tiny window to let in any light. Saroz's mother came in from the kitchen to greet him in the semi-darkness of the stuffy room.

Over the next two hours, Anil told Saroz about Jesus, and then he asked her if she believed what he had shared. With a big smile she said that she did, and she immediately prayed to receive Christ as her Savior. She was eager to learn more, and Anil began to disciple her over the following weeks and months.

As Saroz grew in her faith, she also began to share with her family about Jesus, and she eventually led all seven family members to the Lord. Her home became their church, and Saroz was their leader. She played a drum during their weekly worship service, led the prayers, and taught Bible lessons from all that she learned in discipleship lessons from Anil.

One day, not long after her brother had prayed to receive Jesus, a truck ran him over in the street and broke his leg and pelvis. Without money or opportunity for a doctor's care, the new little church cried out to God for healing. Saroz led the group in fervent prayer, and the Lord answered. Her brother was miraculously healed.

Anil watched Saroz grow in her faith. She was always witnessing, and her commitment to Jesus was unshakeable. Anil soon invited her to receive training to become a church planter. She accepted with joy, and right away she shared the Gospel with her uncle and his family. They also received Christ, and a second church was born with four new believers in her uncle's home.

The next church she planted was in her sister's house. Her sister had come to visit Saroz, and she could not wait to share her good news of salvation. Her sister was amazed at the change in Saroz. She had never seen her so happy. Her sister invited her to come and share the good news with her entire family. Saroz made the trip three days later. Her sister's husband and children, as well as several neighbors, all came to listen. Both Saroz and Anil sang, prayed, and shared from the Bible. That day her sister and four others gave their lives to Christ, and a house church was started in her sister's home.

Saroz was just getting started. Today, her eyes are alive with a passion to tell everyone she knows about Jesus. She bubbles over with all he has done for her and her family, and her faith is wonderfully contagious.

Samita was ready to share her faith with a stranger as she

was going home from the market. Going to the market was just a normal part of her daily life, but when we follow Jesus, a normal day can turn into an amazing connection. Saroz was a person of peace that God put right in Samita's path, and Samita did not miss the opportunity. She could have walked quickly, carrying the weight of her groceries in the heat. She could have hurried home without speaking to a soul. But instead, she took the time to reach out to a fellow stranger on the road, and God used her.

Look for those opportunities as you go through your daily routines. Ask the Lord to help you be alert to the people around you and to look for people to reach out to in friendship. The Lord can make miraculous divine appointments for you just like he did for Samita. Sharing a personal testimony of God's grace in your life can have a powerful impact. Every time we share, we are sowing a seed into the life of a person. The Holy Spirit can use that precious seed to grow faith in a heart and to one day harvest that soul for the Lord.

Samita's simple testimony led to the conversion of Saroz, who soon was obedient to the commandment of Christ to make disciples, and she led seventeen more people to Christ. This conversion also led to the launching of three new house churches. The stream of new believers is continuing still. It's happening all over India. It's happening all over the world. Best of all, we can join the Lord in what he is doing.

The Mechanic

In 2014, an OMS church planter in the Caribbean was riding on a train. He had been taking classes at a seminary and was returning home. He was looking forward to seeing his family again. As always during the journey home, he began conversing with a stranger sitting next to him. This young church planter, who must remain nameless because of security risks, was always on the lookout for potential persons of peace. With his kind and friendly manner, he soon was able to share the difference that Christ had made in his life with the stranger. As his journey was nearing its end, he led the man to the Lord. The old train jerked to a stop, and the church planter realized he was out of time. He apologized and told the brand-new believer that he had to get off the train.

"Wait! What do I do now?" the man asked him.

With no time left, the young church planter just gave the man his Bible and his church-planting manual and said, "I am so sorry to have to leave you, but just read these, and do what they tell you." Feeling dismayed and frustrated, the young man sadly left the train and his new convert, but he faithfully continued to pray for the stranger who had readily received his message and believed.

Nine months later, the leader of the entire OMS church-planting movement in the Caribbean was traveling when his car broke down. He remembered that he had passed through a small village just a mile before, so he began to walk back to the village. As he drew closer to town, he heard singing and realized it was Christian songs he was hearing.

The leader entered the village to find a party in progress with a worship band providing the music. He saw men playing guitars as well as one playing a set of bongos and another playing a large conga drum. The worship was lively and contagious. Men and women were joyfully singing and clapping to the beat. On tables, he saw dishes of black beans and rice, pork sandwiches, chicken and rice, fried plantains, and rice pudding. The town had gone all out for this celebration.

He asked a woman who was nearby to direct him to the town's mechanic, and she replied that the mechanic was the person leading the worship. When the musicians took a break, the leader of the church-planting movement approached the man, introduced himself, and explained that he needed help because his car had broken down. The man's eyes grew large, and his jaw dropped.

"Would you please tell me your name again?" he asked with amazement. The leader repeated his name while a smile grew larger and larger on the mechanic's face. "Nine months ago, I was on a train, and a young man led me to Jesus. But then his stop came, and he had to leave the train. He gave me his own Bible and this book and told me to do what the books said." He proudly held out the worn Bible and the church-planting manual, which had the church-planting movement leader's name right on the front cover. "You are this man, are you not?" Now it was the leader's turn to look amazed; a manual with his name on it had been given to a young church planter, who then passed it on to a new believer who accepted Christ on a train.

The mechanic went on to say, "Today, we are celebrating because we are baptizing two hundred people in the church that the Lord has started here. Please tell that young man that I am continuing to try to do all that I am supposed to. I owe him my life; we all do, in fact. Please, you must stay. It is our privilege to welcome you to this baptism."

The mechanic-turned-worship leader didn't have any formal training as an evangelist, and the young man who witnessed to him on the train had to leave without an opportunity to disciple him. This situation was not ideal, but as a true person of peace, the mechanic continued to follow the Lord through the study of his Word and had immediately begun to refer his whole village to the Lord by sharing all that he was learning. His humble efforts to refer others to Jesus had resulted in dozens more coming to Christ and a large church being formed. His simple faith and testimony had changed an entire village, and the news was spreading even beyond his village to other villages down the road.

The young church planter never dreamed that his chance meeting on a train would result in two hundred souls being brought into the kingdom. An ordinary journey can become extraordinary when we are always looking for persons of peace. Thankfully, this young man had his priorities straight on that important day. He was looking for an opportunity to share his faith and didn't let getting home to his family overshadow his thoughts. The Lord knew he would be faithful to share the Gospel, so the Holy Spirit set up a divine appointment. This appointment was hindered because of a time crunch, but it didn't stop the witness from taking the opportunity to engage the stranger in conversation. Sometimes the Enemy may tell us that there is no time to witness during the busyness of our day, but we must not listen to him. Even a brief testimony that lasts only a moment of time can have major eternal results.

Chapter 6

Instructions from the Master

I n four Gospel passages – Matthew 10:1-42; Mark 6:7-13; Luke 9:1-6; and Luke 10:1-24 – Jesus chronicles his instructions for how we are to do evangelism and how we are to find persons of peace. Jesus did not walk about the countryside alone; he had an organized plan. He chose or recruited people, trained them, gave them responsibilities, and then released them to do the work of the kingdom. Our efforts in the search for persons of peace today will be more successful if we follow the pattern of our leader, Jesus. The Bible is our instruction manual for this ministry. As you will see in this chapter, the Bible gives us all the information we need to prepare ourselves to search for persons of peace.

Prayer Is Our Foundation

Then He said to them, "The harvest truly is great,
but the laborers are few; therefore pray the Lord of
the harvest to send out laborers into His harvest."
(Luke 10:2)

In this verse, Jesus tells the disciples to pray to the Lord, who is in charge of the harvest. This is an important point because it is God who is in charge. The Holy Spirit draws people and convicts hearts of sin (John 16:8). The battle for souls belongs to the Lord, and any results and victories belong to him also. We are his servants who sow the seeds. We must faithfully and diligently put forth the effort so that the lost can hear his Word, but we cannot wash even one person whiter than snow. God alone is in charge of that.

We are instructed to pray for the Lord to send more workers into the harvest fields. It is not God's will for any to perish (2 Peter 3:9). He desires that all should hear of his great salvation. But even with all of our technology and resources, there are many who do not know about Christ in every single nation of the world. We need to pray for more workers to bring the good news. Every Christian needs to be involved in the rescue of the perishing. God's heart breaks as he watches his children remain silent and uncaring or too busy and distracted by the world, while their friends and neighbors face eternity without hope.

Prayer paves the way for God to move. Prayer breaks down strongholds of the Enemy so that the Holy Spirit can do his work. Pray for the lost that you know and will meet. Pray for God to prepare their hearts and create the circumstances needed for them to listen and respond in faith.

Teamwork Is Important

After these things, the Lord appointed seventy others also, and sent them two by two before His face into every city and place where He Himself was about to go.
(Luke 10:1)

Jesus organized his messengers into teams of two, and they did ministry and evangelism together. Jesus knew that one person going alone would become discouraged, tired, intimidated, and likely to drop out before the task was completed. Teams of people can encourage one another and lean on one another for support. They can also provide accountability and give perspective during difficult days. Two or more working together can also accomplish more. One horse can typically pull two tons, but two horses harnessed together have been known to pull twenty-three tons.

Two heads really are better than one for coming up with creative plans and ideas and solving problems in ministry. Often a mature team member can mentor another younger or less-experienced team member. Some examples of mentoring relationships in the Bible include the following:

- Jethro and Moses – Exodus 18

- Moses and Joshua – Deuteronomy 31:1-8; 34:9

- Elijah and Elisha – 1 Kings 19:16-21;
  2 Kings 2:1-16; 3:11

- Barnabas and Paul – Acts 4:36-37; 9:26-30; 11:22-30

- Barnabas and John Mark – Acts 15:36-39;
  2 Timothy 4:11

- Priscilla, Aquila, and Apollos – Acts 18:1-3, 24-28

- Paul and Timothy – Acts 16:1-3; Philippians 2:19-23; 1
  and 2 Timothy

- Paul and Titus – 2 Corinthians 7:6, 13-15; 8:17; Titus

These instructions from Christ Jesus are timeless, and the principle of teamwork is just as important today as it was in the first century. Every believer needs to be nurtured and encouraged by other believers, and they also need to do kingdom work together.

We Are Ambassadors with Authority

Then He called His twelve disciples together and
gave them power and authority over all demons,
and to cure diseases. (Luke 9:1)

Jesus did not send out the teams to journey as weaklings on their own. Jesus sent them out with his full authority. He gave them authority so that they could accomplish their mission with success. Likewise, Jesus sends us forth today representing him. We speak in the authority of his name as joint heirs of the kingdom and as sons and daughters of the King of Kings (Acts 9:27-29).

It is vital that we share the Word of God with people because there is power in God's Word, not in our words (Hebrews 4:12). We can accomplish nothing in our own flesh, but we have authority over the Enemy in the name of Jesus. God has promised us this power (Acts 1:8).

Satan wouldn't have a chance against us if we could only grasp who we are in Christ. Satan wants us to stay feeling weak and powerless. He falsely accuses us constantly because he wants us to live in shame and doubt. It is time to command him to get off our backs and out of our heads and for us to march forward as the saints of the living God. Never forget that we go in the name of the victorious risen Savior.

Read the following verses from the Word of God, and be encouraged to walk victoriously in the knowledge of who you truly are in Christ.

- Alive in Christ – Eph. 2:5
- An Ambassador – 2 Cor. 5:20
- The Apple of God's Eye – Psalm 17:8
- Beloved – Col. 3:12
- Blessed – Deut. 28:1-14
- Called of God – 2 Tim. 1:9
- Changed into His Image – 2 Cor. 3:18
- Chosen – Eph. 1:4
- Complete in Him – Col. 2:10

- Crucified with Christ – Gal. 2:20
- Dead to Sin – 1 Peter 2:24
- Delivered from Darkness – Col. 1:13
- The Elect – Col. 3:12, Romans 8:33
- Established by God – 1 Cor. 1:8
- Firmly Rooted – Col. 2:7
- Forgiven – Eph. 1:7
- Free from Condemnation – Romans 8:1
- God's Workmanship – Eph. 2:10
- Healed by His Stripes – 1 Peter 2:24
- Joint Heir – Romans 8:17
- The Light of the World – Matt. 5:14
- More than a Conqueror – Romans 8:37
- A New Creation – 2 Cor. 5:17
- Overcomers – 1 John 5:4
- Reconciled to God – 2 Cor. 5:18
- Partaker of His Divine Nature – 2 Peter 1:4
- Redeemed – Gal. 3:13
- The Righteousness of God – 2 Cor. 5:21
- A Saint – Romans 1:7, Phil. 1:1
- The Salt of the Earth – Matt. 5:13
- Set Free – John 8:31-33
- Strong in the Lord – Eph. 6:10
- Temple of the Holy Spirit – 1 Cor. 6:19
- Victorious – Rev. 21:7

Supernatural Power Is Available

*And when He had called His twelve disciples to
Him, He gave them power over unclean spirits, to
cast them out, and to heal all kinds of sickness and
all kinds of disease.* (Matthew 10:1)

Acts 1:8 tells us that when the Holy Spirit comes upon us, we
will receive power to be witnesses for Christ all over the world.
As Jesus walked on the earth, he was concerned for both the
spiritual and the physical needs of people. He taught truth and
preached righteousness, but he also had compassion for the sick
and miraculously healed them through the supernatural power
of the Holy Spirit. Through miracles, Jesus fed people when
they had no food, cast out many demons, and set captives free.

Our ministry to people should also involve calling upon
God out of concern for the physical needs of the people we
encounter. *Jesus Christ is the same yesterday, today, and forever* (Hebrews 13:8). He can use us as vessels of healing as we
pray for healing in his name. He can use us to offer food to
the hungry in acts of compassion and kindness in his name.
We can cast out demons through the power of the blood of
Jesus. Miracles and supernatural signs and wonders are still
happening in abundance today through his mighty power.
We must not fear or be shy to approach the King on behalf of
another person. Seeing a miracle can sometimes cause faith to
be birthed in a person's heart.

Trust God to Provide

*And He said to them, "Take nothing for the journey,
neither staffs nor bag nor bread nor money; and do
not have two tunics apiece."* (Luke 9:3)

Jesus told his followers to pack lightly so they could get around
easily and quickly during this short-term mission. The bigger

principle is that this command illustrates that Jesus did not want his followers to be too concerned about accumulating wealth and storing up material possessions. They were to rely on God to provide what they needed on a daily basis, and they were to live in dependence on him, trusting him instead of using their own resources.

Jesus didn't want his messengers to carry anything but a staff, or a walking stick, to protect themselves (Mark 6:8). Through this command, Jesus was explaining that they were to trust in God for their protection as well as for their basic needs for lodging and food. The resources are in the harvest. God would provide the receptive persons of peace to take care of the messengers in their journey.

Sometimes people end their plans for ministry and outreach because the funds are not available or because too many dangers appear. However, Jesus is telling us not to let money or danger stop us when he is commanding us to go. Sometimes we are sent by the Lord and asked to step out by faith even when all of our provisions are not in hand. Sometimes safety has to take a back seat in obedience to a call from God. We must trust God to provide for our every need.

Accept Hospitality

And remain in the same house, eating and drinking such things as they give, for the laborer is worthy of his wages. Do not go from house to house. (Luke 10:7)

Many times God uses other people to provide for the needs of his witnesses. God is weaving plans and purposes through the lives of everyone, both saved and unsaved. Jesus himself said, *"It is more blessed to give than to receive"* (Acts 20:35). The disciples were to accept the food of their hosts graciously and to be thankful. They were not to complain but were to be content with what they received.

Jesus' plan put his followers in the homes of persons of peace so that his followers could spend a lot of personal time with their families. The families who gave hospitality in these biblical testimonies were rewarded with much more than they gave because they received the blessing of the messengers. The families received answers to their prayers for healing and other good things as well. Most importantly, they received the good news of the Master and, therefore, had the best opportunity of receiving salvation through this message.

This teaching of hospitality toward believers continues to be relevant. Those who give a kind welcome to God's messengers and those who allow them to share a word from the Lord will be greatly blessed. They are rewarded to be able to hear the plan of salvation, to be prayed for, and ultimately to receive Jesus as their Savior, which is the greatest blessing.

Search for Receptive People

> *And if a son of peace is there, your peace will rest on it; if not, it will return to you.* (Luke 10:6)

Jesus commands his followers to search for the people who would receive them and the Gospel message. The command is the same today. Jesus came to seek and to save that which was lost (Luke 19:10). He was searching for receptive people, and he requires us to do the same.

Many will not open their hearts to listen to God's Word. Their eyes are blinded, and their ears are deafened. In Jesus' parable of the great feast (Luke 14:15-23), a man has difficulty getting his friends to come to a great banquet, so he tells his servants to *"Go out quickly into the streets and lanes of the city, and bring in here the poor and the maimed and the lame and the blind"* (Luke 14:21). Jesus is clearly showing us in this parable the example of a search-and-rescue mission that we should still be using today.

Jesus also described the search for receptive people as a fishing expedition. He told Peter and Andrew that if they came and followed him, he would make them *fishers of men* (Matthew 4:19). Sometimes results are plentiful and fish just seem to jump into the nets; sometimes results are few and far between.

Our experiences will vary greatly as witnesses for Jesus. But remember, success is not in the numbers of people who respond positively; success is in being faithful all our lives to searching the streets and alleys for those who need the Lord and to throwing out our nets even when the waters are rough and the waves are high. Success is modifying our methods when our search is unfruitful.

Don't Abandon New Believers

Also He said to them, "In whatever place you enter a house, stay there till you depart from that place."
(Mark 6:10)

When the messengers found a person of peace in a village, Jesus commanded them to stay with that family and not move from house to house. Jesus was training his followers to stay and not leave new believers alone after their conversion. The followers also needed to show the persons of peace how to connect to other people in their families and villages so that more people would become believers through their relationships. These persons of peace needed to become a bridge to connect other people to Christ.

This same principle is illustrated in the parable of the sower and the seeds (Luke 8:5-15). A sower went forth to sow seeds. Some seeds fell on the path and were eaten by birds. Other seeds fell among rocks and could not receive water and died. Still other seeds fell among thorns and got choked out. Finally, there were some seeds that fell on rich, fertile soil, and they grew and did well. They even produced a great harvest.

Why did so few seeds survive? The seeds that were left alone to make it on their own, for one reason or another, died. The sower never came back to cultivate, nourish, or protect his precious seeds. A callous evangelist once said, "It's my calling to give the message. After that, it's between them and God." He could not have been more wrong.

Most of our seeds today will not likely fall on fertile soil. These new seedlings probably do not come from wonderful Christian families who have been praying for the new believers. These seeds are probably not linked up with a good church family who will support them. The cultures of our world do not provide a healthy spiritual environment in which new believers can flourish. It is our responsibility as the sowers to follow up with the new seedlings. We are to give our time, our love, and our talents to nurture them in the faith. We have a responsibility to teach new believers the Word so that they can turn right around and teach someone else. By this process, the Holy Spirit can bring in a great harvest for the kingdom.

Shake Off Rejection

"And whoever will not receive you nor hear your words, when you depart from that house or city, shake off the dust from your feet." (Matthew 10:14)

In the culture of Jesus' time, pious Jews would often shake the dust from their feet when leaving Gentile cities to show their separation from Gentile practices and sinfulness. Referring to this custom, Jesus warned his followers ahead of time that not everyone would welcome them. Jesus then told his followers to shake the dust off their feet in Jewish towns where their message was rejected (Matthew 10:14). By using this cultural reference, Jesus was telling his messengers that the people in those towns were not worthy of their message and were deserving of future punishment. He wanted to show a clear separation between those people who accepted the kingdom message and those who rejected the Messiah.

Jesus helped his followers to see that those who hear the message and reject it are responsible for their own choices. He took the blame off the people who share the Word faithfully but do not find persons of peace. Jesus was demonstrating that his followers should not feel responsible or guilty in these instances, because the people are actually rejecting *him*.

The same is true today. We tend to beat ourselves up when we give a witness for Christ without the success of seeing someone brought into the kingdom. We convince ourselves that we are not good at witnessing. Satan can use these thoughts as a way to stop us from pursuing persons of peace many times in the future. Remember that the search for persons of peace is a process, not an event. Studies say that an average person hears the Gospel seven or eight times before he or she makes a decision to follow Christ. You may be only the second person in that person's life to speak about Jesus. Shake it off, leave it with the Lord, and go on looking for the next person to whom you can speak.

Be as Sheep among Wolves

"Behold, I send you out as sheep in the midst of wolves. Therefore be wise as serpents and harmless as doves." (Matthew 10:16)

The phrase *sheep among wolves* has several connotations. Sheep are one of the few animals that do not have any way to defend themselves. Think about it. They do not have claws; they do not bite; they do not kick; and they certainly do not have a hard, protective shell. So if we are to be like sheep, God is telling us that we are not to defend ourselves or to fight back when we are among enemies of Jesus. The Bible teaches that God fights for us (Exodus 14:14).

Sheep are also known for their weakness. Sometimes a sheep cannot even right itself when it falls over. Jesus was not being too complimentary when he compared us to sheep, but he was speaking the truth. Sheep have to depend on the protection of their shepherd when they are among wolves. Sheep must also depend on a shepherd to lead them to water and food. We too must look to God for protection and provision when we are doing kingdom work. The Word of God promises that God will supply all our needs in Christ Jesus (Philippians 4:19). We simply carry on with our work of finding persons of peace who are open and receptive to his message.

In spite of our weaknesses, the Lord sends us today in the same way that he sent out the disciples. We are weak, but he is strong, and he will help us when we encounter difficulties as we search for persons of peace. Knowing our weaknesses as sheep actually helps us because we will depend on God instead of trying to witness in our own strength.

Persecution and Betrayal Will Come

"But beware of men, for they will deliver you up
to councils and scourge you in their synagogues."
(Matthew 10:17)

Jesus said that in this world we would have many troubles, but he also told us to always remember that he has overcome the world (John 16:33). We are told not to be afraid dozens and dozens of times in the Scriptures (For examples, see Joshua 1:9;

Deuteronomy 1:21; Isaiah 41:10). Fear is the opposite of faith. It is an insult to God when we are afraid, because our fear shows that we do not trust him. On the other hand, perfect love for God casts out fear (1 John 4:18). We are never to forget that the ultimate battle has already been won. Our leader is the ultimate overcomer. Our search for persons of peace around this world may lead us into many adventures, but because of God's promises, we do not need to fear what we will say or what will happen to us on our journey.

Jesus' prophetic words were never truer than they are today. There is more persecution of Christians in our world at this time than in all of Christian history. Millions of Christ-followers are suffering great persecution for practicing their faith. In our search for persons of peace, we handle persecution by realizing it is normal for the Christian and expected for the Christian (John 15:18-20). We handle persecution by seeing it as a blessing and a privilege to join in the sufferings of Christ (Romans 8:17).

Betrayal by family and friends is also a possibility. Jesus explained in Matthew 10:34-37 that the truth of the Gospel would sometimes be like a sword, dividing families. It is wonderful when whole families live for the Lord, but often this scenario is not the case. By telling the disciples ahead of time that these things may happen, he was training them and us well. If a teacher does not prepare students for every possibility, he is leaving them unprepared to face what may come.

In many countries, Christians are shunned, disowned, turned over to authorities, or killed when they give their testimony of faith to family members and friends in hopes of finding other persons of peace. Persecution and betrayal may come from those within our closest circles. However, Jesus gives great comfort when he reminds us that even if the worst happens, we are of great value to God, and that is most important (Matthew 10:31, 39).

Love God Most

"He who loves father or mother more than Me is not worthy of Me. And he who loves son or daughter more than Me is not worthy of Me. And he who does not take his cross and follow after Me is not worthy of Me. He who finds his life will lose it, and he who loses his life for My sake will find it." (Matthew 10:37-39)

Jesus ends his instructions to the witnesses with a reminder of the greatest commandment, which is to love God most and to put him first (Matthew 22:36-38). This commandment is our foundational motivation for searching for persons of peace. Our supreme love for the Lord results in a desire to see all mankind reconciled to him. Love for God results in obedience to his commands, one of which is to be a light bearer (Matthew 5:14-15). Our love for him spurs us on to find people who will also worship and obey him as Lord and King.

Jesus teaches that God must take first place in our lives. We must not allow people, possessions, jobs, or any personal desire to take precedence over following Christ in obedience. Galatians 2:20 describes this concept as being crucified with Christ. It states that our lives are no longer our own, and that our will is submitted to the lordship of Jesus. Those who put God first, even at the cost of losing everything, are the ones worthy of our Lord Jesus.

Beware of Pride

"Behold, I give you the authority to trample on serpents and scorpions, and over all the power of the enemy, and nothing shall by any means hurt you. Nevertheless do not rejoice in this, that the spirits are subject to you, but rather rejoice because your names are written in heaven." (Luke 10:19-20)

The disciples were excited when they came back to Jesus to give a report on their mission experiences. They had seen amazing miracles and supernatural phenomenon when they went out doing ministry in his name. Using his authority, people had been healed and demons had been cast out. They returned with triumphant joy, and Jesus also rejoiced in the Spirit and gave thanks to God.

According to the Scriptures, Jesus was also filled with joy. However, he also gave the disciples a warning. He wanted to make sure that their priorities and perspectives stayed true and right. He said that it wasn't the most important thing that they had performed miracles in his name. He did not want them to get puffed up in the success of the moment. He did not want them to become arrogant from the use of the power of God and be tempted to fall because of the sin of pride (Luke 10:17). We are all saved by grace and not our works, so none should boast (Ephesians 2:8-9).

The Lord admonishes us to remain humble in his service (1 Peter 5:5-6) as we go searching for persons of peace and do ministry in his name. Jesus reminded the disciples that our greatest joy should always rest in the fact that our names are written in the Book of Life. In other words, we should always stay grateful that we are sinners saved by the grace of God.

Endure to the End

> "And you will be hated by all for My name's sake.
> But he who endures to the end will be saved."
> (Matthew 10:22)

Our final instruction in the search for the lost is simply to endure to the end. Do not give up the fight. Do not leave the battle for souls. The cost doesn't matter. We will experience rejection. We will have trouble. We may suffer persecution and betrayal. We may lose our families. We may even lose our lives.

Regardless of the cost to us, the mission to seek and to save the lost is more important. We can endure to the end when we put God first. We can endure to the end when we stay obedient and humble. We can keep going in tough times when we keep an eternal perspective and remember that this world is temporary. We can take encouragement from the example of our leader, Jesus, who suffered and died for us. We can be comforted in knowing that we cannot even imagine the spectacular wonders in heaven promised to us and that will never end (1 Corinthians 2:9).

Contained in the instructions in this chapter is everything we need to know to be involved in the search for persons of peace. The instructions are perfect and thorough because they come from Jesus' own teaching. They are pure wisdom and complete nourishment to our bodies and souls. These instructions will indeed enable us to keep searching for persons of peace to the end of our days.

Chapter 7

Parables for Carrying Out the Search

Jesus often used parables to emphasize a truth he wanted people to learn. Parables are stories that use word pictures from everyday life to illustrate an important point. Parables tell a story by using familiar images to represent other ideas. Jesus was a master at using parables. Sometimes his parables were forthright, clear, and obvious; sometimes he used symbolism in his stories to get his message across. Jesus knew his audience, and he knew exactly when and where to use each kind of parable. But ultimately, Jesus was the consummate teacher: he knew how and when to be effective with his Word, which applies today with equal relevance.

In chapter 6, you looked at how Jesus instructed his disciples to go out into the community and find persons of peace. In this chapter, you will learn how Jesus used parables to emphasize how important it is to find people who are lost and to nurture persons of peace among them. From these parables, you will see how important the search for persons of peace is to our Lord.

Luke 15:1-32 contains the following three parables about lost people. In the beginning of this chapter, the religious leaders of Israel were angry at Jesus once again. This time they were greatly offended because Jesus had the audacity to sit and eat with sinners. So Jesus stopped what he was doing and took the time to teach the people through these three parables about their responsibility to search for the lost. These parables contain symbols because the religious leaders had hardened their hearts, and Jesus was trying to get through to them in any way that he could.

The Lost Sheep

In the first parable (Luke 15:3-7), a shepherd left his ninety-nine sheep to go and search for one lost sheep. He kept searching for the lost sheep until he found it, and then he carried it all the way home. He called his friends and neighbors, and they all came and celebrated that he had found his lost sheep.

The sheep represents a lost person, and the shepherd can represent both an individual follower of God as well as the body of Christ as a whole. Jesus is teaching that although participating in activities with your own church flock is easier than going after lost souls, God wants us to spend much of our time going after the wayward, the unlovable, the unclean, and the outcast. In other words, evangelism is our most important task.

Because the shepherd carried the lost sheep all the way home, Jesus is telling us that we need to assist and nurture the newly rescued so that they are protected, cared for, and led to a place of safety where they are welcomed into the community of believers and grow in their faith. This point wonderfully illustrates the necessity of careful discipleship with new believers. As individuals, we must take one-on-one time with the newly rescued to "carry" them along their journey. Study the Bible together. Pray together. Invite them to participate in ministry projects with you. In short, take the time to build a relationship with a new believer.

The shepherd called his friends and neighbors to celebrate the finding of his sheep. Even the angels in heaven celebrated the event. In the same way, we are to celebrate when a lost soul is rescued, because the celebration makes the person feel welcomed and a part of the body of Christ, and it may encourage the person to reach out to others as a person of peace and bring more lost people to a saving understanding of Christ. And so the cycle continues ...

Unfortunately, many churches today do little to rejoice over a new family member. "We have always done it this way" is often the excuse not to change music, traditions, service times, activities, and so on that would be welcoming to a new believer or a person who is lost. Some church members even have the same attitude that the Pharisees had: They don't want to "dirty" themselves by mingling with lost people.

For example, one young minister in the southern part of the U.S. had been witnessing to a known alcoholic who finally came to church on a Sunday morning. The minister was thrilled to see this person in church, to say the least. But after the service, an elderly woman approached the minister and said heatedly, "Well, I guess you'll just let anyone come into our church."

How did this woman get so mixed up about the mission of the church? She actually felt offended when a lost person came through the door. She thought that he would take away the "holiness" of her place of worship. How sad it is that she had been a member of the church for decades but was so mistaken about the purpose of the church. Do you know people with this attitude in your place of worship? The truth is that our churches should be hospitals for sinners, not social meeting places for saints.

How can a church welcome new believers into its midst? First of all, make sure that every new believer is being personally mentored or discipled in the faith. This mentoring must be done in an intentional way or the nurturing needed for growth and strength in the faith will usually not take place. The Gospels show how Jesus spent many hours investing in the lives of the disciples, and today new believers need that same kind of support. When you lead persons of peace into the kingdom, take on the role of a caring and responsible shepherd in their lives and welcome them into the family of God.

You can also encourage your church to have new-member socials. Be sure that you train the members of your church to talk to people whom they don't know and to make strangers welcome. Make the baptism of new believers an exciting celebration in your church body. Be a friendly and welcoming place for all people to come and worship the King. Give new believers a *reason* to invite their friends and family back to your church.

The Lost Coin

In the second parable (Luke 15:8-10), Jesus told the people about a woman who lost one of her ten silver coins. In the custom of that day, a Palestinian woman often received ten silver coins as a wedding gift, so the coins had great sentimental, as well as monetary, value to her. The woman searched and searched for her lost coin. She swept the whole house and even used precious oil to light the lamp so that she could see when the room grew dark. Finally, she found her lost coin, and she was so happy that she called all her friends and neighbors to rejoice with her, just as the shepherd did.

In this story, the coin represents the lost person, and the woman can symbolize both an individual Christian and the church as a whole. Jesus is illustrating in a powerful way that finding lost people is so important that each of us should be willing to work diligently to find them. As lights in this world, we must individually be willing to sacrifice our time, our energy, and even our sleep. Jesus is saying that we should each be willing to spend whatever money it may cost us to search for lost people until they are found.

As a whole, churches sometimes lose their focus on finding and rescuing the lost too. A local Sunday school class was studying evangelism one morning when a class member asked, "How is our church reaching out to the community in evangelism?" An older gentleman replied, "We have a big sign out front that says, 'Everyone Welcome.' So all people in this community know they are welcome here. It's their choice to come or not." What a lazy response that is. Churches need to do more than put up signs to welcome the lost into their midst.

If the coin represents one lost person, then Jesus is showing us how valuable each lost person is. In our churches, we must convey to lost people how important they are in the church community. We should show them how they can become valuable members of the church by inviting them to participate in activities, to attend Bible studies, to become members of small groups – anything that will encourage them to feel a part of the body of Christ and to feel excitement about being a Christian.

When these new believers feel welcome and at home, then they may, in turn, become persons of peace and invite others to church or share the Gospel in other ways. And the stream of new believers continues ...

It is important to involve a new Christian in ministry. Even though they may not know as much about the Bible as some who have been in the church for a longer time, they can certainly share their testimony, and that is instrumental in leading others to Christ. As our stories in this book have illustrated again and again, persons of peace should be encouraged right from the start to use their influence and connections to others and refer them to Jesus.

Try to evaluate your own life as well as your church. How much of your time and energy and money is spent in pursuit of the lost? How much of a priority are they to you? Think about your church. When people share prayer requests, are the lost

mentioned? Is more time spent on fellowship dinners and com-
mittee meetings than on evangelism teams going to search for
persons of peace? Is more money provided in the budget for
beautiful landscaping or vending machines than for missionary
budgets? The true priorities are often reflected in the schedule
of the church and in the budget. Be pro-active in standing up
for the lost in your church.

The Lost Son

In the third parable (Luke 15:11-32), Jesus really wanted to drive
his message home, so he told the religious leaders about the
lost, or prodigal, son. In this story, a young man demanded his
inheritance from his father and left his family. Culturally, this
deed was a rude and arrogant thing to do because it showed
disrespect for the father's authority. The son went out into the
world and squandered his inheritance on wild living. He ended
up so poor that he debased himself by feeding pigs to keep from
starving. For a Jew, feeding pigs was the lowest employment
possible. When he hit rock bottom, he repented, turned from
his sins, came home to his father, and sought reconciliation.

The father began to run to his son when he saw his son coming. The father readily forgave his son and welcomed him back
into the family. He also threw a great party to celebrate his son's
return. But the older brother refused to come to the party or to
welcome the younger brother home. He was jealous of all the
undeserved attention the younger brother was receiving. The
father left the party to come out and tell the older brother that
he should be rejoicing.

In this parable, the younger son represents a lost person;
his father represents God; and the older brother represents a
child of God or the church. Unlike the other two parables, this
parable contains a lost person who purposely abandons God
and the church. After living a life of dissipation, the person

repents and finds his way back to God, only to be rejected by the religious leaders – or the church – of the day.

Jesus wants us to know how much God loves lost people no matter what they do, even if they have actually turned away from him. Jesus shows this love by specifically having the father *run* to meet his son after the son chooses to return home. In that culture, an older man did not run, because running was undignified. But Jesus himself was willing to lay down his dignity and submit to being stripped naked, beaten, and crucified on a cross to show just how much he loves us. God wants lost people to return to him. He is waiting for them to choose to come back.

So if God loves us that much, then shouldn't each of us as members of the church respond in the same way to the return of a lost person to the fold? In the time of Christ, the custom of that day dictated that the older brother should be a mediator between estranged family members. He should do whatever he could to reconcile family members to each other. If the older brother is the church, then Jesus' parable works only if the church is willing to be a mediator between the lost (the younger brother) and God (the father). In other words, the church should do all it can to heal the breach between God and a sinner who has fallen away from his faith. The religious leaders of Christ's time could not bring themselves to accept this teaching, so they rejected Jesus. We need to be sure that our own church authorities apply grace rather than legalism to those who have fallen away from the church.

For example, in a Christian family in Mexico, the teenage daughter became rebellious and ran off with an older man she had been seeing without her parents' permission. She broke off all contact with the family, and they did not know what happened to her. For years, they could not find her, but they never gave up the search. They even hired a private investigator until their money ran out, and they spent many hours in prayer for her safe return.

Several years later, the daughter – beaten and in ragged clothing – came to the door of her family's home. Like the younger brother in this parable, she began to beg their forgiveness, but her voice was soon drowned out by the hugs and exclamations of joy from everyone. Every member of the family praised God for answered prayer, and they loved her and nurtured her back to health. From then on, she was a model daughter and Christian, and the family was forever happy to be reunited.

The biblical parable of the lost son should have a happy ending too. However, Jesus made a stronger point to the religious leaders by illustrating the deplorable attitudes they had toward the lost through the actions of the older brother. The danger with some church members today is in having an unforgiving attitude toward the lost, just like the older brother had in the parable. The older brother, in representing this ungodly attitude, never tried to prevent the younger brother from leaving; he never followed the younger brother; he never tried to find him and bring him back home; and he never welcomed him back. He was callous toward his brother instead of being broken for his lost condition. And when the lost brother came back home, the older brother was the only one who felt no joy. Please be sure that this attitude is not the legacy that you or your church leaves behind.

How can the church help the fallen return to the fold? All Christians need to be willing and ready to go after the lost brother and encourage him to come back. The leaders need to have loving hearts. The people need to be ready to practice forgiveness. The church should provide counseling classes or a mentoring program. All should warmly welcome his return to the Father.

When the church extends grace and love to lost people,

everyone in the church body feels the benefits of that attitude. People feel welcomed and not judged or condemned. A sense of peace and joy permeates the church, and the joy of the Lord flows from its people. When this happens, persons of peace are born because people want others to participate in such a welcoming, pleasant environment. And God's kingdom continues to grow ...

Let us take to heart the message in Christ's parables about the lost. May we exemplify the shepherd who went out after the lost sheep and carried it all the way home. May we follow the example of the woman who worked so hard to search for her lost coin, even sacrificing her time, energy, sleep, and finances. May we be willing to help send someone or to travel ourselves to lands far away to find and rescue wayward brothers. May we help our churches grow and become places where all the lost are welcomed. Let us not stop until we find what was lost.

A Modern-Day Parable

An important Hindu man from India traveled to Dallas, Texas, for a visit. His taxi driver was a young man who was a Christian. As they drove around the city, they passed several huge megachurches with opulent buildings and pristine grounds.

The Hindu asked, "Do Christians really believe that if people do not receive salvation through Jesus Christ, they will receive eternal torture after death?"

"Yes," replied the young man, "that is what we believe."

"No, you don't," the man replied.

"Yes, it's true," insisted the driver. "We believe that all people must be saved through Jesus, or they will go to a terrible place called hell after they die."

"No, you do not believe that," the Indian man said firmly.

"Sir, I don't understand. Why do you keep saying that?" the surprised young man asked.

The Hindu answered solemnly, "There are probably more than ten thousand villages in my own area of India that have not received this information. So I must conclude that either you do not believe what you are saying, or you are truly the most selfish people in the world to keep information that important from the rest of the world. If you really believe what you say you believe, then you should be willing to crawl through broken glass to tell everyone who has not heard."

The driver could say nothing in reply.

Jesus does not want this story to be the final parable of our time. Not only do we have to take the good news to those ten thousand villages in India, but we have to spread the Word throughout the world and in our own country as well. We will need the help of persons of peace whom the Holy Spirit will place in our paths to help complete the mission. Please do not delay in joining the search. Jesus is our model. He has given us the command. He provided our instructions. These biblical, historical, and present-day stories are written to inspire you. There is no time to wait. Persons of peace are waiting for *you*. May the power of the one true God rest upon you and his banner of love overshadow you as you commence your search.

Sources

Allen Roland, *Missionary Methods: St. Paul's or Ours* (Grand Rapids, MI: Wm. B. Eerdmans Pub. Company, 2003).

Gladys Aylward and Christine Hunter, *Gladys Aylward: The Little Woman* (Chicago, IL: Moody Bible Institute, 1970).

"Ancient Roman Governors," *Wikipedia the Free Encyclopedia* (Wikipedia Foundation, May 15, 2013).

Barnabas, "Asia Pacific," *Every Community for Christ Annual Report,* (2012), 8.

Janet and Geoff Benge, *Christian Heroes: Then & Now – Adoniram Judson: Bound for Burma* (Seattle, WA: YWAM Publishing, 2000).

Janet and Geoff Benge, *Christian Heroes: Then & Now – Amy Carmichael Rescuer of Precious Gems* (Seattle, WA: YWAM Publishing, 1998).

Janet and Geoff Benge, *Christian Heroes: Then & Now – Hudson Taylor Deep in the Heart of China* (Seattle, WA: YWAM Publishing, 1998).

William Blair and Bruce Hunt, *The Korean Pentecost.* (Great Britain: Banner of Truth Trust, 1977).

Blair, William Newton, *Gold in Korea* (Topeka, KS: H.M. Ives and Sons Inc., 1957).

Robert Bradshaw, "The Life and Work of Adoniram Judson, Missionary to Burma," *www.theologicalstudies.org.uk* (1992).

Interview with Deanna Cathcart, One Mission Society, March 20, 2013.

Vance Christie, *Into All the World (Heroes of the Faith)* (USA: Barbour Publishing Inc., 2004).

Dave and Ann Dedrick, "Walking with Cemetery," *OMS Outreach*, Vol. 111, No. 1 (Jan.-April, 2011), 4.

Lillian Dickson, *These My People* (Grand Rapids, MI: Zondervan Publishing House, 1976).

LeRoy Eims, *The Lost Art of Disciple Making* (Grand Rapids, MI: Zondervan Publishing House, 1978).

Terri England, *Slavery in the West Indies in the 18th Century* (Chronicle Barbados, Roots Web. 2002).

David Garrison, *Church Planting Movements* (Midlothian, VA: WIGTake Resources, 2004).

"Jonathan Goforth China's Greatest Evangelist," History Makers, *www.history makers.info/Inspirational-Christians* (accessed December 14, 2012).

James E. Kiefer, "Lars Olsen Skrefsrud, Missionary to India," Lutheran Kalendar, Biographical Sketches Of Memorable Christians of the Past, *http://justus.anglican.org/resources / bio/16.html* (Society of Archbishop Justus, August 29, 1999).

Carolyn and Phillip Knight, *God's Love Still at Work. Still At Work Series, Vols. 1 and 2* (Florence, MS: Stephen's Printing, 2005).

Life Application Study Bible (Wheaton IL: Tyndale House Publishing Co., 2004).

Interview with Jonathan Long, One Mission Society, March 20, 2013.

Jason Mandryk, *Operation World, 7th edition* (Colorado Springs, CO: Biblica Publishing, 2010).

"Modern Day Mt. Carmel Power Encounter," *OMS Outreach*, Vol. 109, No. 3 (Sept.-Dec. 2009), 15.

George Patterson and Richard Scoggins, *Church Multiplication Guide* (Pasadena, CA: William Carey Library, 2002).

George W. Peters, *A Biblical Theology of Missions* (Chicago, IL: Moody Press, 1972).

Don Richardson, *Eternity in their Hearts* (Ventura, CA: Regal Books, 1981).

B. A. Robinson, "Caodaism (Kingdom of Heaven) A Vietnamese Centered Religion," *www.religious tolerance.org./world religions* (October 7, 2009).

"Searching for a Person of Peace," *OMS Outreach*, Vol. 109, No. 3 (Sept.-Dec. 2009), 14.

David Smithers, "Count Zinzendorf and the Moravians," *Awake and Go Prayer Network.*

Randy Spacht, "Doing Whatever it Takes, Fulfilling the Great Commission in Five Ways," *OMS Outreach*, Vol. 111, No. 1 (Jan.-April 2012), 4.

Vlad Soshkin, "The Spirits of Mozambique." 2010-2011, Colorful Crazy World Vlad Soshkin Photojournalist, *www.vladsoshkin. com/projects* (May 14, 2013).

Lester F. Sumrall, *Through Blood and Fire in Latin America* (Grand Rapids, MI: Zondervan Publishing House, 1944).

Jean Pierre Tabo, "Church Planted in a Day," *OMS Outreach*, Vol. 112, No. 1 (Jan.-April 2012), 12.

"Tayal of Taiwon." Joshua Project US Center for World Mission, People in Country Profile, *www.JoshuaProject.net/people profile.*

Pierre Tristan, "Muslim Imam," *www.about.com/middle east issues* (December 6, 2008).

Doris Trefen, *From Headhunters to Halleluyahs* (Chattanooga, TN: AMG Publishers, 1980).

Ruth A. Tucker, *From Jerusalem to Irian Jaya* (Grand Rapids, MI: Zondervan Publishing House, 2004).

"Wa," *www.encyclopedia.britannica.* Encyclopedia Britannica online. Encyclopedia Britannica Inc. 2013, Web 17, May 2013.

Waddington, R. "The Lahu People." Peoples of the World Foundation, *www.peoplesofthe world.org* (accessed May, 16, 2013).

Sam Wellman and Gladys Aylward, *Heroes of the Faith* (Uhrichsville, OH: Barbour Pub. Inc., 1998).

Interview with Rich Yoder, One Mission Society, March 21, 2013.

K. P. Yohannan, *Come, Let's Reach The World: Partnership in Church Planting Among the Most Unreached* (Carrolton, TX: Gospel for Asia Books, 2004).

K. P. Yohannan, *Revolution in World Missions* (Carrolton, TX: Gospel for Asia Books, 2004).

Marcus and Alyxius Young, "Our History," *www.divineinheritance.com/t our history-white*

Donkey.aspx (2008).

Rad Zdero, *The Global House Church Movement* (Pasadena, CA: William Carey Library, 2004).

About the Author

Dr. Carolyn Knight was mentored in evangelism at an early age by her father. She served as a pioneer evangelist and church planter in East Africa for ten years and has personally experienced the results of finding persons of peace. Today, she assists in facilitating church-planting movements in Asia with Every Community for Christ (ECC), and is a trainer for new missionaries at One Mission Society. Carolyn is the founder of Light in Darkness Ministry, a ministry rescuing women working in the sex industry. Carolyn has a passion to inspire and empower Christians to share their faith. For more information or to schedule a personal evangelism workshop for your church or other group, contact Carolyn at cknight@onemissionsociety.org.

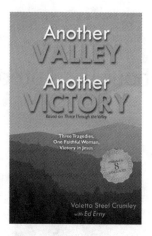

Valetta lost her young son Danny to leukemia; her husband Henry succumbed to Hodgkin's disease a few years later; then she lost her remaining two children in a tragic car accident. Her new reality was nearly unbearable, but when offered a secure position in her father's business, Valetta refused. The Lord had called her and Henry into ministry, and there was a mountain of unfinished business.

Today, Valetta has traveled the world, sharing Christ and teaching Christians how to share Christ in their communities. Thousands have been saved, and countless more inspired in their walk with the Lord. Valetta's story will touch you, move you, and challenge you to let God do as he desires in and through your life, enabling you to minister to others in ways you never would have imagined possible.

OMS · ONE MISSION SOCIETY

NO RESERVES, NO RETREATS, NO REGRETS

The Life and Ministry of Ed Erny

Ed Erny

My life story begins with a preacher who, by the leading of the Spirit, refused to end a service until my father, a successful businessman, had given his heart to the Lord. I eventually followed in my father's footsteps into full-time ministry, but only after overcoming self-doubt and self-consciousness in my ability to share the gospel.

God took that doubt away when a young man gave his heart to the Lord after I told him about Jesus. From that moment on, in Taiwan, the Philippines, and other places where I served, I saw the tremendous hand of the Lord at work as I allowed Him to lead and work through me. My desire is that you will be inspired and motivated to serve the Lord as freely and willingly as I was privileged to do for many years. May you, by God's grace, determine to live with no reserves, no retreats, and no regrets.

ÔNEMISSION
OMS · ONE MISSION SOCIETY

Young Men of the Cross is the story of One Mission Society's commitment to do something never before attempted—to place the Gospel message in every home in a nation. Their target was Japan, which at the time had 10.4 million homes. The Great Village Campaign was launched in 1913 with young Japanese evangelists carrying Scriptures to thousands of homes on small islands, in dense forests, and across barely accessible mountain ranges. In 1917, ten young men from God's Bible School in Cincinnati volunteered to work with the Japanese evangelists to complete this monumental task.

The Second Crusade, a sequel to *Young Men of the Cross*, tells of One Mission Society's post-World War II attempt to again reach every home in Japan with the gospel. This time, the program was called the Every Creature Crusade (ECC, now known as Every Community for Christ), and young college students joined national coworkers in spreading the gospel in Japan. Later, crusaders were sent to Korea, Taiwan, and Hong Kong to take the ECC program to those OMS fields as well. One OMS leader said of the effect of the ECC in his life: "As our crusade team moved from town to town and witnessed the salvation of hundreds and the planting of scores of churches, it was this more than anything else that drew many of us back to those fields as career missionaries."

OMS · ONE MISSION SOCIETY

Hidden Treasures

Missionary life is not what most people expect. One Mission Society missionary Millie Young shares in her biography, *Hidden Treasures*, that it is so much more than just preaching. Making daily contact, organizing camps, running Christian schools, and living among the people are vital components of ministry. It is letting the local people see you living your life, overcoming obstacles, and laughing. Millie experienced hardship and provision, joy and heartbreaking sadness, insurmountable obstacles and immense success in spreading the salvation message to the lost—especially in the rural areas of Colombia. Her missionary work is the living legacy of changed lives.

ONE MISSION
OMS · ONE MISSION SOCIETY

Benjamin Franklin once wrote that the two certainties of life are death and taxes. But for the Christian, certainty is so much more. *Faith is confidence in what hope for and assurance about what we do not see"* (Hebrews 11:1). By faith, with *No Guarantee but God*, Charles Cowman, Ernest Kilbourne, and Juji Nakada embarked on an adventure with God that began a missionary organization in Japan in 1901 that today spans the globe.

For more than five decades, Enrique Guillen has lived out faithful obedience to the Great Commission with an audacious, persistent trust in the power and provision of God. He has consistently modeled how to train emerging leaders and release them for effective ministry. This is Enrique's story … but it can also be yours! *One Faith Multiplied* is more than a biography; it includes opportunities for you to learn how to integrate Enrique's examples into your own life and ministry.

OMS · ONE MISSION SOCIETY